SMALL CLAIMS COURT
Making Your Way Through the System
A STEP-BY-STEP GUIDE

OTHER RANDOM HOUSE LAW MANUALS

Using a Lawyer
. . . And What to Do If Things Go Wrong
A Step-by-Step Guide

Probate
Settling an Estate
A Step-by-Step Guide

Real Estate
The Legal Side to Buying a House, Condo, or Co-op
A Step-by-Step Guide

A RANDOM HOUSE PRACTICAL LAW MANUAL

SMALL CLAIMS COURT

Making Your Way Through the System

A STEP-BY-STEP GUIDE

THERESA MEEHAN RUDY
in Association with HALT

RANDOM HOUSE NEW YORK

All rights reserved under International and Pan-American
Copyright Conventions. Published in the United States by Ran-
dom House, Inc., New York, and simultaneously in Canada by
Random House of Canada Limited, Toronto.

This work was originally published in different form as *Small
Claims Court* by HALT—An Organization of Americans for
Legal Reform, in 1981 and in 1988.

HALT is a national, nonprofit, nonpartisan public interest
group with more than 150,000 members. Based in Washington,
D.C., its goals are to enable people to handle their legal affairs
simply, affordably, and equitably. HALT's education and advo-
cacy programs strive to improve the quality, reduce the costs
and increase the accessibility of the civil justice system. Its
activities are funded by members' contributions. The original
draft of this book was authored by Paul Hasse and Chip Green-
wood. Substantial assistance with this book was provided by
Dennis St. George, Timothy J. Wall and Richard Hébert.

Library of Congress Cataloging-in-Publication Data

Rudy, Theresa Meehan
    Small claims court: making your way through the system:
a step-by-step guide/Theresa Meehan Rudy in association
with HALT.—Rev. ed.
        p. cm.—(A Random House practical law manual)
    Includes bibliographical references.
    ISBN 0-679-72950-X
    1. Small claims courts—United States—Popular works.
I. HALT, Inc. II. Title. III. Series.
    KF8769.Z9M44   1990
    347.73'28—dc20
    [347.3074]

Book design by Charlotte Staub

Manufactured in the United States of America
Revised Edition

Contents

Introduction

The small claims court is a court of law that considers only noncriminal matters. It is called "small claims" because it usually settles money disputes involving a few thousand dollars or less.

A small claims court operates according to rules that are far less complicated than the procedures of other trial courts, and for small claims, a growing number of states are doing away with the technical language and legalistic forms normally associated with going to court. Like other courts, small claims courts have a judge and, at rare times, even a jury, and an increasing number also operate arbitration or mediation programs that try to resolve problems before they reach the courtroom. Finally, although rare, small claims cases may even involve lawyers representing one or both sides.

This book will help you answer the following questions:

• Should I go to small claims court with my problem?
• If so, how do I present my case to the court?
• If I'm sued, how do I defend myself in small claims court?

Before answering any of these questions, you must know something about how small claims courts operate. You must also be able to recognize the types of cases that a small claims court will and will not consider. Finally, you must be able to apply the rules of your state's courts to your particular problem.

This basic preparation will help you determine if your case meets the "entry requirements" of the small claims court in your state. If it does, you must then decide if going to a small claims court is the best way to resolve your problem. You may find that you can get a better solution outside the court. What kinds of situations are handled in small claims court? Here are a few examples:

- A dry cleaner ruins a jacket and refuses to pay for it.
- A landlord will not return a security deposit.
- A dog owner won't compensate a neighbor for the damage caused by a dog bite.
- An appliance store won't repair or replace a dishwasher that repeatedly breaks down.
- A building contractor fails to seal a roof properly.
- A motorist dents someone's fender and doesn't have insurance to cover the damage.
- A retailer, repair person or professional cannot collect on an overdue bill.

Small claims courts allow consumers to resolve small but important money disputes quickly and inexpensively. When small claims courts are available, consumers are afforded greater access to courtroom resolution without the need for full-fledged litigation. If the number and location of small claims courts were increased as well as the dollar limit allowed, the public would be better served.

A WORD ABOUT TERMS

This book uses common, everyday language. Fortunately, not a great deal of technical language is used in small claims court. Where familiarity with a legal term can be helpful, however, a plain-language definition of the legal word or phrase is also included in this book. Knowing these few legal terms can help you complete forms more easily and deal with clerks and judges more effectively.

Appendix IV is a glossary of legal terms. Many of these terms do not appear in the text but are included because they are used in Appendix I.

HOW TO USE THIS BOOK

This book offers information that you must know to secure your rights in small claims court. Careful use of this book won't guarantee you a victory, but it will prevent you from ruining your chances because of mistakes that could have been avoided.

Read the text for general information and then refer to the appendices at the back for specific information about the rules and resources in your state.

Whether or not you initiate the suit, you should also know about alternatives to lawsuits (Chapters 1 and 2); the legal basis for a suit (Chapter 3); how to file a legal claim (Chapter 4); the rules for *service of process* (Chapter 5); and how to collect your evidence and present it in court (Chapters 8 and 9). If someone is suing you in small claims court, refer to Chapters 6 and 7 for specific methods of defending yourself.

COURT PERSONNEL AND LAWYERS

If, after reading this book, you still have questions about your case or need more information about local procedures, ask the clerk in small claims court for help. These clerks realize that most cases brought into small claims court will be presented by the people involved and not by attorneys.

Although small claims court clerks are usually more willing

to offer help than the clerks of other trial courts, they still feel the threat of bar prosecution for giving "unauthorized" legal advice. Because of this, some may refuse to give you anything more than the most basic information.

If you have questions that cannot be answered by this book or by the small claims court clerk, don't assume you have to hand your case over to a lawyer. You may want to consider hiring a lawyer as a *pro se* coach or consultant to answer your specific legal questions, to review legal documents or to make suggestions. If you do need this kind of help, find a lawyer who will agree to work under such an arrangement and to charge a reasonable hourly rate.[1]

[1]For tips on hiring and using lawyers, we suggest *Using a Lawyer* by Kay Ostberg in association with HALT, Random House, 1990.

SMALL CLAIMS COURT
Making Your Way Through the System
A STEP-BY-STEP GUIDE

CHAPTER 1

BEFORE COURT

Small claims courts offer a relatively quick and inexpensive way to settle disputes. Still, you should be aware that, although pursuing a small claims case does take less time and money than would be required for a formal civil trial, a small claims suit will probably require at least two trips to the courthouse during business hours—once to file the appropriate papers and once for the hearing. And if you encounter postponements or problems with collecting a judgment, you could be forced to make as many as four or five return trips.

Quicker, less expensive and often more effective methods for resolving small claims are also available even *before* you go to court. Not only can these alternatives save you time and trouble, they will also greatly strengthen your case if you are forced to go to court. Judges in small claims courts expect both sides in a dispute to make every reasonable effort to resolve their problem before resorting to court action. If you can demonstrate that you sought peaceful resolution but the other side refused to communicate, cooperate or act in good faith at all points before the hearing, your chances of victory will be greatly increased.

The following suggestions may seem basic, but it is important to follow them carefully. Remember that you are not only complaining—you are also methodically building a case.

THE TELEPHONE CALL

The first step in seeking a remedy to your problem should be a businesslike telephone call to whoever is responsible for it. Before you begin, have a pen and paper at hand, plus notes about your case—names, dates, the amount of money in dispute, and so on. What you say will depend on the nature of the problem, but the form of the conversation should be as follows:

1. Identify yourself and your address. If you have dealt with the other side previously (for example, if you are calling a company that didn't repair your roof properly), give your name as it might appear on their records: "This is Mrs. Elizabeth Jones of 321 Baker Street."

2. State the reason you are calling. Don't explain it, state it. Don't waste your explanation on a receptionist and don't allow yourself to be sidetracked.

3. Ask to speak to the appropriate person—whoever has the authority to offer an immediate remedy. It's extremely important that you deal with the right person from the beginning. If the problem involves a child, you'll want to speak to the parents. If it's a small business, speak to the owner. If it's a large store or manufacturer, ask to speak to the customer service manager.

4. Identify yourself again and your problem. This time, follow up with the question: "Are you the person responsible for handling this sort of problem?" Get a definite answer before you continue.

5. Ask for the name and title of the person with whom you are speaking. *Write this down.* Ask for the correct spelling of the name. This will assure that you'll have a record of whom you spoke with and that a follow-up letter, if necessary, will go to the right person.

6. Describe the problem. Keep your description as brief as it would be in a short business letter. Refer to your notes so you can be sure you are being accurate.

7. Make a firm demand. State precisely what you expect to be done about your problem. Be polite, but be firm. (Example: "I expect your repairmen to be out here tomorrow to seal this roof properly, or I want all of my money back. Moreover, I expect compensation for the water damage to my carpets and wallpaper.")

8. Get an answer. Don't accept "I'll have to think about it" or "Maybe we can squeeze it in next week" or "See the manufacturer," or mumbo jumbo about "implied warranties." You need a specific promise or a clear refusal to rectify or compensate you for the damage or injury done. Without this, the telephone call has been a waste of time. Don't be rude, but persist until you get a "yes" or "no" answer. ("Then you will send somebody out tomorrow? And you'll pay for any damages not covered by my insurance?")

9. Set a deadline. Agree to a schedule and expect the other side to meet it. When that deadline has passed, it's time to move to the next step.

THE FIRST LETTER

With any luck, one letter may resolve your problem. If it doesn't, it will help convince the judge that you behaved reasonably at all times and made a sincere effort to resolve the matter before going to court.

The letter should be similar to your telephone call: concise, unemotional and firm. It should be no longer than one page. It should be a succinct record of what happened.

Always use plain English and avoid legal terms or you may say something you didn't mean and end up sounding foolish.

Most important, write so the letter and therefore the dispute can be clearly understood by a disinterested third person.

The disinterested third person may turn out to be the company president, a representative of the manufacturer, a Better Business Bureau official, an arbitrator or ultimately a judge. Such persons, particularly judges, will not have the time or inclination to read an eight-page tirade about your woes. They will simply want to know who, what, when, where and how much. Don't worry about boring the person you're writing to by recounting the facts. It's important to remember that your letter may become a "minibrief" for that disinterested third person.

These third persons will also want to know if you have behaved reasonably throughout this difficulty and if your account of the situation can be believed. Their verdict will depend in part on the reasonableness of your demands. It will also depend on the tone and length of your letter. Anyone who cannot get to the point in one page and refrain from name calling and exaggeration will be treated with skepticism if not ignored completely. After a judgment of this sort, your chances of success are greatly reduced.

Your first letter should be straightforward. Again, the content will depend upon the dispute, but your letter probably should include these points:

1. *The right addressee.* Send the letter directly to the person you spoke with on the telephone. If you handled the telephone call properly, he or she should be the person in charge and the one who made a commitment to you.

2. *The date, nature and location of the incident.* To refresh your correspondent's memory and to establish the facts for the future, briefly describe your cause for complaint. Be sure to include the names of all those involved, such as salespersons and repairpersons.

3. *The broken promise.* Here you must establish, morally and legally, that the other side is responsible for your difficulty. If you purchased goods or services, you did so with a reasonable expectation of getting your money's worth. If you gave your landlord a security deposit, you expected to get it back after leaving the apartment in good condition. If your neighbor's dog bit you, you reasonably expect the owner to accept responsibility for the failure to keep the dog confined.

4. *Your efforts to resolve the problem.* Mention your telephone call and the failure to respond adequately to your complaint. Describe any commitments made on the telephone and say why they failed to satisfy you.

5. *Your demand.* This demand may or may not be the same as the one made over the telephone. If the response to your first demand was insufficient, you may want to draw the line here. Keep your final demand simple and reasonable: for example, ask that your money be refunded, or insist on compensation for the damages you suffered.

6. *A reasonable deadline for compliance with your demand.* In most cases two weeks will be perceived as reasonable.

7. *Don't make threats.* This is not the time to threaten legal action. It will make you seem unreasonable and eager to invite conflict. Moreover, it's poor strategy. One mention of legal action may leave you speaking with the legal department instead of customer services.

A good letter should look like the sample that follows:

Mrs. Elizabeth Jones
321 Baker Street
Midland, MI 33242
Tel.: 438-2614
January 5, 1990

Mr. T. Williams
Hottin Roofers, Inc.
26 Tobacco Road
Midland, MI 33242

Dear Mr. Williams:

On November 20, 1989, I hired your firm to repair the roof of our house at 321 Baker Street. On November 21, two men from Hottin Roofers (a Mr. Bates and another man with a large mustache) arrived and began repairs. They worked for two days. I received a bill for $1,650 and paid it in full on December 7, 1989.

It rained on December 13. The roof leaked at the exact spot where the "repairs" were performed, and there was substantial damage to the carpet and wallpaper below. When I hired your firm to repair the roof, I was promised high-quality repair work. The job performed by your employees clearly fails to meet this standard.

When I called you on December 14, you refused to send someone to seal the roof, and you refused to discuss compensation for the damage caused by the leak. Given the circumstances, I think the only way to settle this matter is for you to refund the $1,650 I paid Hottin Roofers, plus $350 to cover the deductible for my homeowners' insurance policy. I expect a check from Hottin Roofers within 14 days.

Sincerely yours,
Mrs. Elizabeth Jones

cc: Homeowners' Insurance Company

Type your letter. Just as no third person will take the time to read an eight-page letter, few, if any, will bother trying to decipher your handwriting. Also, typed letters look more serious and businesslike.

Make several copies of the letter. You'll need copies for your files, for other interested persons, to include with your second letter, and for the judge or arbitrator. Photocopies are better than carbons.

Send the original of the letter by certified mail, return

receipt requested. Besides getting the attention of the person you're writing, this will prevent that person from claiming that he or she never received the letter.

Send copies to all *interested* third persons. At this stage, send copies only to those who are actually involved in the original incident or who have a direct financial or legal interest in the resolution of your dispute. In Mrs. Jones's case, for instance, she should notify her insurer that she has contacted Hottin Roofers about compensation for that portion of the damage not covered by her policy.

When other persons also suffered damages, they should be notified. For example, if you and a friend were bitten by a neighbor's dog, send a copy to the friend. But that's it. Don't overdo the "cc" tactic. Some people "cc" everyone from the White House to their suburban newspapers. Not only is this unnecessary, it often destroys the credibility of the person complaining.

Now wait. If you gave the other side fourteen days to reply, wait the full fourteen days. Don't start calling or sending updated versions of your first letter. You may make yourself appear unsure of the merits of your claim. You may also make it possible for the other side to claim that you changed the demands contained in your original letter.

Start a file. You don't need anything elaborate, but you do need a folder, envelope or box to hold all correspondence, invoices, canceled checks, names of witnesses, estimates of damage and the like.

THE SECOND LETTER

If you don't get an answer to your first letter, or if the other side makes a counterproposal you think is inadequate, write a second letter. This one should be even briefer and precisely to the point:

                                         Mrs. Elizabeth Jones
                                         321 Baker Street
                                         Midland, MI 33242
                                         Tel.: 438-2614
                                         January 19, 1990

Mr. T. Williams
Hottin Roofers, Inc.
26 Tobacco Road
Midland, MI 33242

Dear Mr. Williams:

Two weeks ago I wrote to you and asked for a refund of the $1,650 I paid Hottin Roofers to fix our roof. I also asked for $350 to compensate for the damage done when your "repair" failed to prevent the roof from leaking. You have not responded to my request. [*Or:* I don't think your offer of $500 is sufficient.]

I still believe a full refund plus the $350 is the only fair and reasonable way to resolve this matter. If you do not make a reasonable settlement offer in the next week, I shall be forced to take further action. Please contact me immediately.

                                         Sincerely yours,
                                         Mrs. Elizabeth Jones

Enc: My letter of 1-5-90
Your reply of 1-11-90 [if any]

cc: Homeowners' Insurance Company
    Better Business Bureau
    XYZ Homebuilders Association

Warn that you may take "further action," not "legal action." For all the reasons mentioned in discussing your first letter, you still don't want to seem too eager to rush into courtroom combat. Plus, it's still important to keep all your options open at this stage. Even if it is possible to take your case directly to small claims court, you may have a better chance of getting what you want through alternative dispute resolution procedures. (Your options—and when you should consider using them—are discussed in the next chapter.)

Be sure to enclose a copy of your first letter and the reply, if you received one. Also include these copies if you "cc" any interested third persons. Again, send the letter by certified mail, return receipt requested, and keep a copy for your files.

If you are dealing with a supplier of goods or services, it may help to send a copy of your second letter and all enclosures to the Better Business Bureau, the Chamber of Commerce or a relevant local trade association. Always attach a note to copies of your letters and explain to these organizations that you will be seeking help if the matter cannot be resolved otherwise.

These organizations probably will not do anything about your problem simply because you've sent a letter. You usually have to file a formal complaint to guarantee assistance. This procedure is discussed in the next chapter. However, it is important to let your opponent know that such organizations are being informed. The merchant may feel safe in ignoring you, but he or she can't ignore the risk of a bad reputation in the business community.

If you bought an appliance from a retailer, send a copy of your letter to the parent company that sold the retail franchise, plus a copy to the manufacturer of the product you bought. A letter to these companies often results in direct action. To get their addresses, consult a business directory at your local library. Start with *Standard & Poor's Register of Corporations, Directors and Executives.* It contains information on more than 50,000 American business firms. If you know the name of the product but don't know the corporate name of the manufacturer, look in the *Thomas Registry,* available at your local library.

CHAPTER 2

ALTERNATIVES

Sometimes you can't take your problem to small claims court. If a dog keeps digging holes in your yard and you want the owner to keep the dog on a leash, small claims courts in most states cannot help you. You could seek money for the damage the dog caused, but in this type of dispute, nuisance and aggravation are more the issue than money. Small claims courts can't settle long-running family or neighborhood disputes, and they can't prevent future problems. In all but rare circumstances, they can award money only for proven damages.

Small claims courts also cannot hear cases in which the amount of money sought exceeds the limit set by state law. You should claim as much as you can justify but never more than the dollar limit allowed (see page 45.) The limit ranges from $1000 to $5,000. More than half of the states have set their small claims court dollar limits between $1,500 and $2,500. In the example used in Chapter 1, Mrs. Jones would not have been able to sue Hottin Roofers for $2,000 in the small claims courts of fourteen states. (Though to get into small claims court, Mrs. Jones could reduce her claim to $1,500 since that is her state's dollar limit.) Check Appendix I for the dollar limit in the small claims courts in your state.

If your dispute cannot be settled by paying you money or if the amount of money in question exceeds your state's limits, you will be forced to seek alternatives to small claims court. You may also want to try these alternative resolution measures even if your claim is eligible for consideration in small claims court. Sometimes the best strategy is to stay out of court—or to use the court as a last resort.

Most of these alternatives are tailored to particular types of disputes. If your dispute fits within one of these categories, the alternative procedure may well give you the quickest, least expensive and most satisfactory solution. The remainder of this chapter discusses these alternatives and the types of problems they deal with.

CONSUMER ACTION AGENCIES (CAAs)

Consumers often buy goods and services whose value exceeds the dollar limits set by their state's small claims courts. If you buy a major appliance or a car or hire a contractor for home improvements or repairs, it is unlikely that you will be able to take a "full refund" demand to your small claims court.

Even if you can sue, it may be better to take your complaint first to a consumer action agency (CAA). Most small claims courts can offer only cash awards, and you may want something else—such as a replacement, new parts or a prompt repair job. Also, suing a large company can be complicated and time-consuming.

Registering a complaint with a CAA, on the other hand, is simple, and the agency will do most of the work for you. Another advantage is that large companies are more likely to cooperate with a CAA than to respond to the possible threat of a small claims trial.

CAAs are classified by the manner in which they are funded and operated. Some are run by government, some by private consumer groups and some by business and individual groups. Note that all of these will expect you to have made a personal effort to resolve your dispute (for example, by the telephone call and two letters discussed in Chapter 1) before turning to them for help.

GOVERNMENT CONSUMER ACTION AGENCIES

Most states have consumer action agencies at the state, county and city levels. These offices are familiar with local and state laws and will either help you directly or refer you to the proper agency.

Many complaints are handled at the local level. Call your local office and ask that a complaint form be sent to you. Fill it out and return it with copies of supporting documents such as sales slips, other sales documents and whatever correspondence you've had with the merchant. (Most offices will accept a written letter with supporting documents in lieu of their complaint form.)

After your complaint is filed, an investigator will be assigned to your "case." If additional information or an on-site investigation is needed, you will be contacted. When the information is compiled, the investigator will negotiate with the merchant in an attempt to reach a mutually agreeable solution. This may take several exchanges of telephone calls and letters.

Some areas have strong consumer protection laws that empower the CAA to take legal action against merchants if necessary. They can negotiate cease-and-desist agreements, issue subpoenas and civil citations and file lawsuits. Not all consumer protection offices have this kind of clout, however.

If your area has no city or county consumer office, try the state office. Some states have a separate consumer affairs office, while others have it within the governor's office, the attorney general's office or both. Appendix III lists the addresses and telephone numbers of state consumer affairs offices.

If your dispute concerns the sale of professional services, state licensing and regulatory boards may be able to help. Doctors, funeral directors, lawyers, electricians and hundreds of other professionals must meet licensing standards set by state agencies. These agencies often handle consumer complaints and can bring disciplinary actions. However, the usefulness of filing such a complaint varies from profession to profession and from state to state. Before spending a lot of time taking a complaint to a licensing board, check with your local private CAA or a consumer affairs reporter at a local television station to see if the effort is worthwhile.

Federal agencies usually have their own consumer affairs office. Most provide general information but only a few (notably the Post Office) investigate individual complaints. For more information on the various federal agencies and the types of matters they will consider, write for a free copy of the *Consumer's Resource Handbook,* Consumer Information Center, Pueblo, CO 81009.

PRIVATE CONSUMER ACTION AGENCIES

All states and the District of Columbia have private consumer groups that may operate at the local as well as state level. These are usually staffed by volunteers and can give you information and advice on how to handle your problem. These groups usually don't have the authority to force a resolution, but they can put you on the right track and are an invaluable source of information about local business practices.

To locate private consumer groups in your area, check with your state or local government consumer office or call a local television news department and ask for the consumer affairs reporter. If these sources can't help you, contact national consumers' groups like the Consumer Federation of America or the National Consumers League, or try the Division of Consumer Organizations in the U.S. Office of Consumer Affairs. Their addresses and telephone numbers are listed in Appendix II.

MEDIA PROGRAMS

Some newspapers and many TV stations help consumers with a "hot line" or "action" service. If your efforts (the telephone call and the two follow-up letters) don't get a response, find out if your area has a media-sponsored consumer action program. Media programs of this sort are often successful because the businesses involved act quickly to avoid bad publicity. You can find out if your community has such a media-sponsored program by simply calling your local newspapers and radio and TV stations, and asking if they have a consumer reporter.

BUSINESS CONSUMER ACTION AGENCIES

Both local business communities and national industry groups also sponsor consumer action programs. Like media programs, these tend to get quick results because the offender wants to avoid getting a bad reputation with colleagues, competition and prospective customers. Filing a complaint with a business CAA is a good first step because if they are unable to resolve your problem, you can still take your case to small claims court. The three most important business CAAs are the Better Business Bureaus (BBBs), Consumer Action Panels (CAPs) and trade associations. Addresses and telephone numbers for the last two are listed in Appendix II.

Better Business Bureaus

BBBs are nonprofit organizations organized and funded by local and national businesses. Most of the 180 BBBs in the United States offer general consumer information, including records of previous complaints against individual companies.

The national office reported that BBBs received 11.5 million consumer inquiries and complaints in 1988. Home improvements, service firms, and retail sales ranked as the three areas that received the most inquiries "from consumers seeking to check out the reliability of individual companies and various offers before buying."

BBBs accept written complaints against a business and will contact the firm on your behalf. They will help you settle the case until you are satisfied or the company can convince them your claim is unjustified. Some BBBs also offer binding arbitration if all other attempts at resolution fail (see "Arbitration," page 18.)

Consumer Action Panels (CAPs)

As consumer awareness spread during the early 1970s, several industries initiated consumer action panels to handle consumer complaints. Two industries still have such panels: the automobile dealers (AUTOCAP) and the makers of major home appliances (MACAP).

Upon receipt of a complaint, the panel writes a formal letter to the manufacturer or dealer asking for an explanation of the problem and encouraging a resolution that will satisfy the customer.

If the problem is not settled after a fixed period—usually a week to 10 days—it is brought before a review board composed of industry and consumer representatives. The board studies the file and recommends a solution.

While these recommendations are not legally binding, a manufacturer may be prodded into agreement rather than face trade association sanctions. The consumer is free to pursue remedies elsewhere if dissatisfied with the panel's decision or the results. Since it is always in the interest of a business to have a clean record, the panels achieve a high rate of success. In 1988 MACAP resolved to consumers' satisfaction approximately 77.2 percent of the 645 complaints it received.

Trade Associations

Many national trade associations can handle consumer complaints, but not all have consumer action panels. This does not necessarily reduce their effectiveness, however.

Local trade associations have been created in some communities by auto dealers, homebuilders and others. Some of these associations investigate consumers' complaints, but they were formed primarily to protect their members' interests and only a few are truly aggressive about helping consumers. To find out if a relevant trade association exists in your area—and if it's worth approaching them with your problem—contact a local consumer action agency or consumer affairs reporter.

Two notes of caution: whether you're taking your dispute to a BBB, a consumer action panel or a trade association, remember that each of them has restrictions on the types of cases it can handle and that their effectiveness is reduced when the manufacturer or dealer you are complaining about is not a member of the industry group that sponsors the program.

ARBITRATION

Resolving disputes through arbitration is often easier and more satisfactory than appearing in court. The technique of arbitration is as old as Solomon, but its use has grown dramatically in recent years. It is now used extensively by businesses in labor contract negotiations. Lately, courts have also moved to make arbitration available for settling minor disputes in both criminal and civil matters.

In arbitration, the two disputing sides appear for a hearing before a neutral third party who listens to arguments, considers the evidence and makes a decision. It is similar in many ways to the small claims court procedure. In practice, however, arbitration is even simpler than small claims procedures. Little paperwork is involved, and formal rules of evidence don't apply. When and where hearings are conducted is often determined by the preferences of the two sides and the arbitrator. This allows quick, easy and informal proceedings, which are particularly helpful when on-site inspection is needed to arrive at the truth.

Arbitration is almost always voluntary: both sides must agree to it and agree beforehand to accept the final decision of the arbitrator. Once arbitration is agreed to, the two sides select an arbitrator, usually an expert on the type of problem at hand. Sometimes a panel of three or more arbitrators is required. The agency sponsoring the arbitration, usually the Better Business Bureau (page 20) or the American Arbitration Association (page 21), will give you a list of arbitrators and an explanation of the rules.

The hearing is informal and conducted in a private, relaxed atmosphere. You'll be able to state your case and ask questions of the other side. The arbitrator may also ask questions and may have arranged for an expert witness to present additional information. Lawyers are permitted at the hearings in most cases, but this depends entirely upon who is sponsoring the arbitration.

The arbitrator will try to encourage the two sides to come to agreement. If this is not possible, the arbitrator's final decision will be made within a set period of time—usually ten days. The decision is written, binding and enforceable by the courts.

Depending on the rules, you may or may not be able to

appeal the arbitrator's decision, so be sure you know the rules before you begin.

Arbitration has several obvious advantages beyond the speed and ease of the process. For example, an arbitrator has more flexibility than a small claims judge; the arbitrator can decide that a service—and not a cash award—is required. Also, both sides may be asked to do certain things to effect the resolution, whereas a judge is limited to deciding which side should be required to make restitution. Further, arbitrators are not subject to the dollar limits that are imposed on small claims court cases.

Several different agencies sponsor arbitration. The following descriptions should help you determine which forum best suits your needs.

Better Business Bureaus

The Better Business Bureau operates the National Consumer Arbitration Program in more than 140 major metropolitan areas. The BBB's arbitration program handles only consumer business disputes. It excludes personal injury and property claims, allegations of fraud and violations of criminal law.

The BBB pays for the cost of its arbitration, and the arbitrators usually are local volunteers—businesspeople, homemakers, educators, lawyers and doctors. You and the other side will be allowed to help choose the arbitrator for your case.

As mentioned before, when you approach the BBB with a complaint, it will first try to settle it by contacting the business and asking that the complaint be resolved. If this fails, the BBB will offer arbitration if it's available in your area.

If the other side agrees to arbitration, the BBB will explain the rules and help you arrange a hearing. This is a simple, inexpensive and highly recommended method of resolving otherwise difficult consumer problems. Contact your local

Better Business Bureau to see whether arbitration is available in your area.

American Arbitration Association (AAA)

The American Arbitration Association (AAA) is a nonprofit public service organization dedicated to resolving disputes. It has thirty-three regional offices around the country. For a local address and telephone number, check your telephone directory.

Using the AAA has both advantages and disadvantages. It can handle cases concerning large sums of money without limits. Also, it considers a broad range of problems not handled by the BBB. And, as an independent organization, the AAA may be more flexible in meeting the special needs of your dispute.

The primary disadvantage is the cost—the fees charged by the AAA to arbitrate a case are based on a sliding scale. Cases involving up to $25,000 require a 3 percent administration fee, with a $300 minimum charge. This is paid by the side that initiated the complaint, but apportionment of the costs may be included in the arbitrator's final award. Cases over $25,000, but less than $50,000, require a 2 percent administration fee with a $750 minimum charge. Between $50,000 and $100,000, it's a 1 percent administration fee with a $1,250 minimum charge.

Court-Sponsored Alternative Dispute Resolution (ADR) Programs

Today all courts, especially those with a heavy backlog of cases, promote the use of alternative dispute resolution (ADR) programs. ADR is an umbrella term used to describe a variety of nonadversary, out-of-court techniques for settling disputes. The best-known examples are mediation and arbitration.

If you're lucky, the small claims court in your area sponsors an arbitration or mediation program. Alaska, California,

Connecticut, Illinois, Louisiana, Maine, Massachusetts, Michigan, New York, Ohio, Oregon and the District of Columbia each has a small claims court that refers cases to mediation or arbitration (see Appendix I). Several other states also offer mediation or arbitration programs at higher court levels.

The procedure for getting your case to arbitration varies from state to state. For example, in New York City litigants are asked when they appear in court if they are willing to have an arbitrator hear and decide their case. If they agree, they immediately meet with a volunteer lawyer serving as an arbitrator. In California the arbitration of small claims cases within a given monetary range is voluntary for the person bringing the suit, but if he or she opts for arbitration, it becomes compulsory for the person being sued.

Small claims courts in some areas of Connecticut, New York and Ohio have compulsory arbitration for all disputes within a certain dollar range. In many places, New York City for example, arbitration is faster and simpler than litigating the dispute, but the arbitrator's decision is final: you cannot appeal.

Maine, Massachusetts, the District of Columbia, and some districts in other states offer mediation for small claims (see "Mediation" below). Mediation relies on the two sides involved to reach a mutually agreeable settlement. If mediation results in a written agreement entered into the case file, it is binding and enforceable by a court.

In the District of Columbia small claims are referred directly to mediation through a pilot project called the Multi-Door Dispute Resolution Program that matches people and their problems to the most appropriate dispute resolution mechanism. The program, sponsored by the American Bar Association, is part of a nationwide effort to relieve court congestion by increasing the availability of alternatives. Multi-Door programs have also been established in Boston, Massachusetts, Houston, Texas and Tulsa, Oklahoma.

MEDIATION

The first mediation programs in the United States were created in the late 1960s and early 1970s. At that time mediation was almost exclusively used at the community level to resolve problems between family members, neighbors and local businesses and their customers. Community-based mediation enjoyed so much success that it caught the attention of courts, legislators and private and governmental agencies, all of which eventually explored the possibility of instituting mediation programs.

Mediation works best among persons who will have an ongoing relationship after the dispute is settled. That's why many small claims disputes are easily mediated. The dry cleaner has a vested interest in keeping customers, neighbors usually must continue to live next to each other and immediate family members, for better or worse, will continue to see each other.

Mediation is voluntary and informal. The parties do not need to submit evidence or bring witnesses. Each side simply tells its version of the story. If they cannot agree on what the main issues or problems are, the mediator meets with each party separately.

Once problems and issues are listed, the mediator uses a variety of communication skills to get the two sides to come to an agreement. The mediator asks questions, discusses areas of compromise, and may even make suggestions; but a good mediator does not impose a decision, as an arbitrator or a judge would. The final decision is made by the parties themselves, not the mediator.

Once agreement is reached, it is put into writing and signed by both sides. Like any contract, the agreement is legally binding and enforceable in court. If you do not like a proposed agreement, you cannot be forced to sign it. If you have questions about the meaning or validity of an agreement, you should ask a legal professional to review it with you *before* you sign it.

Mediation programs are offered at the community level, through some local courts, and by independent private mediators. Court-sponsored mediation was discussed in the previous section. Brief descriptions of community and private mediation follow.

Community-Based Mediation

Dispute resolution centers (also called neighborhood justice centers) were first developed to reduce the burden of courts handling minor civil and criminal disputes. They have done just that and, at the same time, have provided a quick and inexpensive alternative to court. More important, they can often confront and deal with the underlying problem between two parties—not just the official accusation that is the focus of a particular case. Examples of such cases include juvenile vandalism, neighborhood noise disputes and police-community relations.

More than 400 dispute resolution centers currently operate in the United States. There are also many private practitioners who provide services to courts and communities. Each center has its distinct purpose and its own rules of procedure. The major differences among the dispute resolution centers involve: (1) the type of disputes handled; (2) the sponsorship and funding of the project; (3) the method of resolving disputes; and (4) the types of mediators and arbitrators used.

Private Mediation

The growth of private dispute resolution services in recent years can be attributed to the public's dissatisfaction with the expense and delay of traditional litigation.

Private mediation is offered through organizations like EnDispute in Washington, D.C. and Chicago; American Intermediation Services in San Francisco; the Center for Public

Resources in New York City; and Dispute Resolution, Inc., in Hartford. Mediation groups like these provide full-time mediators who encourage the other side to participate and also offer extensive follow-up services. Many of these groups mediate disputes involving amounts of money well above small claims court limits.

To learn more about community or private mediation services in your area, you'll need to do some telephoning. Try your city attorney general's office, the small claims court clerk, the mayor's office, local consumer groups or your local bar association. You can also check under "Mediation Services" in the yellow pages or write to the Standing Committee on Dispute Resolution, American Bar Association, 1800 M St. N.W., Washington, DC 20036. The ABA's Standing Committee acts as a clearinghouse of information on alternative dispute resolution and it also publishes a *Dispute Resolution Directory* that describes hundreds of community-based mediation programs.

CHAPTER **3**

DO YOU HAVE
A CASE?

If alternative dispute resolution procedures are not available in your area, if they are not applicable to your problem, or if they fail to produce an acceptable settlement, it's time to consider taking your case to small claims court. At this point, you must answer two questions: Is your dispute eligible for small claims court? and Do you have a case?

The first question is relatively easy to answer. Your dispute is eligible if it involves less than the dollar limit set by law for small claims courts in your state and if it does not involve an issue specifically excluded from the court, such as libel or slander. The way to calculate the amount of your claim will be discussed later. For the moment, check Appendix I of this book to see if there are any obvious reasons why your dispute might be excluded from your state's small claims courts.

The second question—Do you have a case?—is not so easy to answer. You should begin by examining your state's eligibility requirements. Besides restricting the amount of money at issue and the type of cases heard, most states also restrict settlements to cash awards. In other words, whatever loss or damage you have suffered, whatever rights have been violated, you must ask the court for compensation in the form of a specific amount of money. For example, you cannot ask the court to order the defendant to replace your

26

Waterford chandelier with the exact model, but you can ask that you be compensated in cash for the value of the chandelier you lost.

Restricting settlements to cash awards enables judges to process small claims cases more quickly. Faced with hundreds of cases a week, judges naturally seek to reduce problem solving to a simple formula. This formula generally includes four basic questions: *What happened? Who did it? Were they wrong? How much did it cost?*

Remembering this formula will help you determine if your case is the sort that the court, in *any* state, prefers to handle. Cases that involve a landlord who refuses to return a security deposit are easily decided by the formula. The two sides in the dispute are known; the amount in dispute is clear; the landlord will offer reasons for failing to return your money, and, if the judge finds the reasons unacceptable, the amount and form of compensation are obvious: a cash payment of the amount of your deposit.

Dog bites and falls on icy sidewalks also account for many cases on small claims court dockets. However, beyond medical bills and damage to your clothing, it can be difficult to prove that any other damages should be translated into cash. Other elements, such as pain and suffering, inconvenience and annoyance, introduce value judgments that are not welcomed by small claims court clerks and judges. Such factors are included in some cases, however, and will be discussed later. Just remember that small claims judges simply prefer cases that involve specific damages that can be easily documented and resolved by a payment of cash.

The second thing to keep in mind is that, in most states, small claims court is a court of law and not a court of equity. That means a judge cannot give a ruling based solely on what he or she deems is "fair," but must rule based on the law, regardless of how unfair the results may be. In most states that means you can win only if the judge can "apply the law to the facts." For example, if you can provide written evidence that you sold your car "as is," it doesn't matter if it breaks down on the buyer that same week. The judge will have to rule in your favor because you have written proof of a legal and binding contract—whether that seems fair or not.

In small claims courts, the judge will not expect you to know the law. In fact, she or he will probably resent any attempt you make to argue fine points of law. Instead, you will be expected to tell your own story in your own words. When you present your case, deal only with the simple facts about what happened and don't get into probing and legal diagnosis.

If you are aware of the basic questions and issues the judge is trying to resolve, you can and should emphasize the important aspects of your case by bringing appropriate evidence. Knowing the underlying legal structure of your case will help you marshal your factual evidence in a way that will do the most good. For example, if you're a landlord trying to evict a tenant, you should be aware of what the grounds for eviction are—damage to property, disturbing the peace and nonpayment of rent are just a few. Knowing this allows you to come to court prepared with convincing evidence— pictures of or actual damaged property, neighbors who will testify about noise levels or bounced checks that prove rent hasn't been paid in months.

The remainder of this chapter discusses the legal questions you must answer to "prove" your case and the types of verdicts allowed by law. Because small claims court judges have a fair amount of leeway in making decisions, the following discussion cannot be definitive. It can only serve as a guide to help you organize your presentation in court.

Basically you must answer only two questions. The first: Have you suffered a loss that can be documented in court? The second: Is the person you are suing liable (legally responsible) for your loss?

DID YOU SUFFER A LOSS?

The emphasis on dollar limits and cash awards points to one of the essential elements you must prove in court: loss of other elements—pain and suffering, for example, can enter a small claims suit only on the coattails of a solid case that documents *monetary* loss.

In six states, judges are not so narrowly restricted. In those states a judge who believes your claim is justified may order a specific act to be performed by the person being sued, if that seems to be the fairest way to resolve the dispute. For example, a judge in one of those six states could order someone to return a one-of-a-kind object if merely paying for it wouldn't be adequate. This will be discussed further, but it's worth noting here that to get into small claims court, *you must assign a dollar value* to your dispute regardless of what outcome you want. As a result, your case will still be limited to the maximum dollar amount the court is allowed to consider.

IS ANYONE LIABLE?

Loss is not the only element you'll have to prove. The other is *liability*—the law's way of establishing blame and determining responsibility. The problem is not as simple as discovering who did or didn't do the act that started the dispute. Rather, you must answer: "Is the defendant liable?" That is, did the person you are suing do something wrong— or fail to do the right thing—and *did that act cause your loss?*

Bear in mind that someone can do something wrong and not directly cause you a loss. For example, your neighbor may have ruined your plans to run errands in the morning because he boxed your car in with his. This doesn't mean you can hold him responsible for a car accident you had while doing your errands in the afternoon. You can't claim that the accident wouldn't have happened if he hadn't boxed you in earlier. Your neighbor's action was not the direct cause of your car accident.

The "wrong" you must demonstrate is what will interest the judge, who will want to answer at least one of these three questions:

- Was the defendant negligent ("wrong" by not acting carefully or responsibly)?
- Did the defendant commit the act intentionally ("wrong" by willfully causing you harm)?
- Did the defendant break a valid contract ("wrong" because of a broken promise)?

If the "wrong" falls into one of these three categories and you can demonstrate that it caused your loss, the defendant is liable and should be required to make restitution. Once the facts are determined, it's as simple as that. But facts can sometimes be difficult to pin down.

Was the Defendant Negligent? Establishing negligence or willful wrongdoing can be more complicated than it might seem. A standard often used is what is called "reasonable care," the degree of precaution that should be expected from anyone under similar circumstances. If you can show that the person you are suing failed to act with reasonable care, in effect you show that that person acted recklessly or negligently and is therefore responsible for the damages the careless action caused.

For example, a driver who is speeding in a residential area and plows into a child's bicycle would undoubtedly be found guilty of "negligent behavior." But negligence may be—and often is—attributed to either or both sides in a small claims suit. Not only defendants, but persons who bring suit have a basic obligation under the law: they must have acted responsibly to reduce the loss.

This means that when you accuse someone else of negligence, the judge may be equally interested in how you behaved. If the person you are suing can prove you also were negligent or failed to act responsibly to reduce your loss, the judge must compare the consequences of your acts and those of your defendant. In the example we've just seen, the driver could claim that his own safety as well as the safety of others was endangered because the bicycle was lying in the middle of the street and he had to hit it to avoid hitting someone or something else.

In the case of Mrs. Jones and Hottin Roofers, Mrs. Jones was responsible for preventing further damage by sealing the roof and mopping up the water as soon as possible. If she let the water stand for days, or suffered further damage when it rained two weeks later, the judge will want to know why she didn't do something to prevent part of the damage.

When both sides are partly responsible, the judge may apply the legal doctrine of comparative negligence or contributory negligence depending what state rules apply. Under "comparative" negligence, the judge assigns each party a percentage of the blame and applies it to the claim. For example, if you sue for $500 and are found responsible for 10 percent of the damage, then the defendant's 90 percent responsibility will entitle you to $450. Most states apply comparative negligence.

"Contributory" negligence is less kind to people who sue: if you are negligent in any way, you cannot recover anything from the party you are suing. In the few states that use contributory negligence, you may be allowed to raise additional defenses to eliminate your own contribution to the damages you suffered. For example, if it can be shown in an auto accident case that even though both parties were at fault, the defendant had the "last clear chance" to prevent the accident from happening, an opportunity the plaintiff didn't have, then the plaintiff's share of negligence could be eliminated.

Say, for example, that Joe Plaintiff drives through an intersection at 8 P.M. without his car's headlights on. Sally Defendant, in a hurry to get home, runs a stop sign and sideswipes the back end of Joe's car as he is making his left turn. Joe will claim that Sally is at fault for running the stop sign. Sally will say she didn't see Joe's car because he didn't have his headlights on and therefore he is partly at fault. Joe could counter with the "last clear chance" doctrine: that he was well into his turn and didn't have time to get out of the way, but that Sally had plenty of time, judging from where she hit his car, to prevent the accident if she had just applied her brakes. In this example, Sally would not succeed in shifting the blame to Joe.

Was the Harm Intentional?   Even though your loss is the same through intentional or accidental acts, the amount you can recover will be more if you can prove that the wrong committed against you was intentional. For example, if you can prove that a neighbor drove over your fence and knocked down your tree because he doesn't like the fact that your son is dating his daughter (and not because his steering wheel locked and caused him to swerve into your property) you can ask the judge to award additional "punitive" damages. The total amount you ask for, however, cannot exceed the small claims court dollar limit.

Has a Contract Been Broken?   Most small claims cases involve contracts. This might surprise you unless you know that a contract does not have to be written to be binding. You enter into oral contracts all the time (hiring someone to cut your lawn or paint your house, selling personal belongings at a garage sale, renting out your basement as storage space, ordering goods through the mail). For most matters that arise in small claims court, a good working definition of a contract is "any agreement that involves an exchange of promises or a promise exchanged for some act or compensation."

When a contract is in dispute, even if it was never written down, the judge's task is fairly simple. Evidence will be asked about the terms of the contract, how it was created and whether it was actually agreed to and is binding on both sides. If the person you are suing failed to keep a promise and loss or damage resulted, the judge will order that person to compensate you. Say, for example, you offer to sell your stereo to a friend for $800. She accepts by paying $400 now and promising to pay $400 by the end of the month. The end of the month comes and goes without any payment. When you call to ask for the balance she comments that $400 was more than enough for your stereo and slams down the phone. You sue her for breach-of-contract even though you never asked her to sign anything.

Most contract disputes in small claims courts involve breach-of-contract or fraud. In breach-of-contract cases, the person who sues claims that the contract is valid and should be enforced. In fraud cases, the person who sues claims that the contract is *not* valid and should *not* be enforced.

In breach-of-contract cases, you are saying that the person you are suing has failed to fulfill the obligations as agreed to in the contract. This requires you to prove three things: a valid contract existed, that it was broken and that as a result, you suffered a loss. Proving this follows a fairly straightforward path. The technique for preparing and presenting a convincing case will be discussed in Chapters 8 and 9.

A judge also has the power to rule that a technically legal contract is nevertheless invalid because it is grossly unfair or fraudulent. An example of a legal but unfair contract would be a landlord's rental agreement that charges twice the going rate for rent to a non-English speaking immigrant. Fraud is the misrepresenting or concealing of facts with the intent to deceive and thereby gain advantage over another person. In a suit based on fraud, you will have to prove that an important fact was knowingly concealed or lied about (for example, that the odometer had been rolled back on a car advertised as having "low mileage" or that the papers on a prize-winning Doberman are false). Proving fraud can be difficult, given the limits on time and evidence in small claims court. Because most fraud cases are also subject to criminal prosecution, if you think you have a case that involves a fraudulent contract, check with your city or county district attorney's office before filing suit in small claims court. If the district attorney's staff decides to prosecute, it will collect evidence, and perhaps win a conviction, that will make it easier for you to collect your small claim.

"Fairness" is a less common reason for overturning contracts. In such cases, a judge decides that the circumstances, experience, knowledge and sophistication of the people who entered into the contract were so unequal that the contract, though technically complete, should be canceled. Judges are reluctant to do this, however, both in deference to the legal principle of *caveat emptor* (Latin for "let the buyer beware") and because defendants usually appeal when judges rule that their contract was "unfair."

WHAT WILL YOU "WIN"?

What all small claims courts have in common is their ability to settle disputes by ordering payment for proven losses or damages. What varies from state to state is the maximum amount of money the injured person is allowed to claim (see Appendix I).

As we've seen, however, six states also allow small claims judges to order the defendant to do something other than simply pay you money. These states are said to allow "equitable relief." Their small claims judges are said to have "equity powers." In plain language, "equity" means "fairness."

If fairness demands that the only way to compensate you is to require that a specific act be performed for you, the judge with equity powers may so order. For example, you may have sold an antique that you would like to have returned because the other side refuses to pay. In six states, small claims judges have the authority to order the return of your antique.

In another nine states, small claims courts have *limited* equity powers. Judges in these courts are limited in what they can order either side to do. In North Carolina, for example, the judge has no equity powers except to order enforcement of a lien. In Tennessee the judge's power is limited to issuing restraining orders.

In those states whose small claims courts have no equity powers, the judge can only order that you receive the payment you agreed to.

Remember that even where it's allowed, it is the judge's option, not yours, to offer equitable relief. If the judge feels that a cash award is the best way to settle your case, you will have to accept the money. Check Appendix I to see if your state's small claims courts allow equitable relief.

Judges in states that do not officially offer equitable relief may encourage remedies that look very much like it. If a cash settlement appears to be a poor way to solve your problem, the judge may be willing to suggest solutions "off the record," before deciding on a verdict. He or she may suggest that you and the person you are suing step into the hall to "work things out." If you can't, the judge will have to award a money damage. If you can, you might get money and a promise that the problem won't happen again—for example, reimbursement for geraniums that were destroyed by the neighbor's dog and a promise that the dog will be kept on a leash or behind a fence.

The chances of getting something other than a cash award in small claims court depend partly on your state's laws and partly on the whim of the judge. You shouldn't count on getting noncash relief any more than you should count on getting the full amount of money you're asking for. This is why, if money clearly won't solve your problem, you should seek arbitration or mediation rather than going to small claims court.

To learn if the judge in your local small claims court allows or encourages anything other than cash awards, check with the courthouse clerk. Explain the sort of resolution you'd like to see, and ask if it is possible. Then ask if it's likely. The second question really concerns the judge's preferences in verdicts, and only a clerk—or your own observations in the courtroom—can provide an answer.

CHAPTER 4

FILING SUIT

$\mathbf{Y}$ou now have an idea of what a qualified small claims dispute might be: you have suffered a loss, someone else is liable, and you think you can prove it. The next step is to make sure you file your complaint properly. Since each small claims court has its own administrative process, established through local rules, it's a good idea to ask the court clerk if a brochure is available that describes how the process in your area works. Though the brochure won't be thorough, it will tell you what the local procedure is for filing a suit and may also tell you whether the rules of the court have been revised recently. (For example, the dollar limit may have been raised.)

You can probably get a copy of the brochure by calling the clerk's office and asking that one be mailed to you. The name of the small claims court in your state is listed in Appendix I of this book, and the telephone number of the nearest courthouse will be in your local telephone directory. If you have to pick up the brochure at the courthouse, bring your documents with you and plan to file your suit while you're there and save yourself a trip.

When you file suit, you will have to pay a filing fee, usually $5 to $10 but sometimes as high as $35. You will also have to fill out a form called the "Plaintiff's Statement" or "Statement of Claim" or some variation of these. The name varies from state to state. Some states also require a second statement, called a "Declaration under Penalty of Perjury," in which you swear that everything you've stated is true. Others simply have you sign the Plaintiff's Statement. Either way, you are responsible for the truth of any statement you make. The forms for Plaintiff's Statements vary among states, but they seek the same basic information: your name, whom you are suing and the amount you are seeking.

Answering these questions properly can be more difficult than it appears. This chapter will help you avoid making technical errors, but if you have any questions that are not answered here or in the court's brochure, ask the court clerk.

Small claims court clerks are generally helpful and will try to answer most questions if they think you've made a serious effort to prepare in advance. In some large metropolitan areas (such as New York City, Chicago and Los Angeles) trained paralegals or legal assistants may be available to help you. If your case is unusual or complicated or involves a large sum of money, you may also want to seek legal help (see Chapter 7).

Before you can complete the Plaintiff's Statement, you'll need enough information to answer the questions that follow. Try to get these answers by telephone or a trip to the library before you spend an afternoon running back and forth to the clerk's office.

WHERE SHOULD YOU SUE?

The court's legal term for where you should sue is "venue," the locality in which a case may be tried. This is established mostly for the convenience of the two sides in the dispute and is left to the discretion of the judge.

To decide where to sue, you first need to know how the small claims court system in your state is subdivided. You may be allowed to file suit in more than one small claims district. If so, you'll need to decide which you prefer.

Each small claims court has its own district, with specific geographic boundaries. New York City has several districts, but most small claims districts encompass an entire city, several cities or even an entire county. Only occasionally— as in Louisiana, Montana, Oregon and Pennsylvania—do the rules and dollar limits vary among the districts within a state. If you live in such a state, examine your case and the resolution you're seeking. You may be able to choose a district where one or more of the variations works to your advantage. For example, if your case involves a relatively large amount of money, you may want to sue in the district with the highest possible dollar limit. If your state has no variations, or if they don't matter, choose a district with the proper venue that is most convenient to you.

The questions of choice arises because state requirements usually indicate where you *can* sue rather than where you *must.* Courts often have the power (jurisdiction) to take a case within a wide geographic area. Start by checking Appendix I of this book to see what your options are. Regardless of which state you live in, you can always sue in the judicial district where the defendant lives or does business at the time you file suit. This rule anticipates the defendant's objection that it is too inconvenient to appear.

The defendant's proper address shouldn't be too difficult to find. Look first in the telephone book, then in city registers or directories, police files and tax records. These records are usually kept in or near the courthouse where you file your Plaintiff's Statement. If you're naming a business in your suit, some states specify that you must give the address of the business headquarters rather than simply the "place of business." If you're suing a large national company that has many offices, you may be forced to file suit somewhere other than where you did business.

The odds are that you won't have to go to great lengths

to track down your defendant. In more than thirty states, you can sue where the injury or damage occurred. With a contract dispute, it's where the contract was signed or, in some states, where the act specified by the contract was to be performed. Thus, most retail or service companies—even if they are a franchise operation of a national corporation—will have to face you in a local small claims court. Another option, available in only a few states, is suing in the district where the defendant was living or doing business *when the contract was created.*

Problems you might encounter in trying to serve your defendant with the Plaintiff's Statement may also influence your choice of where to sue. Some states require that the defendant be served in the small claims district in which the suit is filed, so be sure you read Chapter 5 before making a final decision on where to sue.

WHOM SHOULD YOU SUE?

Always sue the person, persons or business that harmed you. If the offenders are married, you must sue both. Whenever you sue more than one person, be sure to name them individually. The Plaintiff's Statement will have space for you to name more than one person. List each name and address separately.

Cars and Motorists   You should always check to see if the driver of an auto is its legal owner. If the driver of a vehicle is not its registered owner, in most states you must sue both. The owner's and driver's names should be available from the accident report if one was filed with the police. If not, give the state department of motor vehicles the license number, explain why you need the information and ask for the registered owner's name. If a business owned the vehicle, sue the driver *and* the owner(s) of the business.

Minors   If the offender is a minor, you must name a parent or legal guardian as well. In such cases, liability varies from state to state, but often a child's actions must be shown to be "willful misconduct" before a parent will be judged automatically liable. Laws may also limit the damages that can be recovered from minors. For example, in most states minors cannot be held to contracts they have signed. For other matters, the parents probably are liable and you should name them.

Businesses   If you're suing a business, you need to determine whether it is owned by an individual, a partnership or a corporation. If the business is not incorporated, find out who owns it and sue "[owner], d.b.a. (doing business as) [name of business]"—for example, John Smith, d.b.a. Smith Roofers. To find the owner's name, check the premises for a business license or try the records at the city or county tax offices. Finding the owner's name is crucial because unincorporated businesses *cannot* be required to pay a judgment. Your state's court rules will specify how complete a name you must use (for example, whether the first and/or second initials are acceptable). The clerk should be able to answer your questions, but if you're having trouble finding the owner's full name, the name he or she generally uses is usually enough, unless it's a nickname.

Partnerships   All partners in a business are individually liable for the acts of that business, so you should find and name each partner separately, besides naming the business itself. Failing to name all partners (for example, if some of them live out of state) will not disqualify you, but it will result in fewer people from whom to collect should you win a judgment.

Corporations   Corporations are "persons" for the purposes of legal action. Individual officers are usually not liable for the debts of the corporation, so you must concentrate on finding the exact legal name of the corporation. Don't assume that the name on the door of a company is the corporate name. For all you know, "Jake's Cleaners" may be legally incorporated as "International Cleanomatic Corporation, Inc." To determine the right name, try checking the business license office, tax records or the local or state office that supervises corporations, usually the secretary of state.

Every state except California requires you to sue a corporation under its corporate legal name. As a practical matter, however, you shouldn't worry too much about this because you will usually be permitted to amend pleadings (your Plaintiff's Statement) if you get the name wrong.

Public Officials   If the offense was committed by a public servant acting in an official capacity, that person is probably shielded by the regulations of the city, county or state agency. If this is the case, you must sue the public body—and deal with entirely different problems. Some states prohibit all small claims suits against government agencies or their employees. If you are allowed to sue, you probably won't be able to get the officials to court until you've filed a claim with the agency and followed all agency procedures established for such disputes. The agency may take what seems to be forever to review your claim, but you must wait until the process is completed before you will be allowed to bring suit in small claims court. And if you finally get to court, don't be too optimistic about your chances of winning. Your opponent will, where it's allowed, probably be represented by an attorney from the government agency, and the judge will be inclined to protect the interests of local or state government.

WHO IS SUING?

Many of the same rules about properly identifying defendants also apply to you as the plaintiff. If you are not the only one suing, all plaintiffs' names and addresses must be included on the Plaintiff's Statement. Only one of you needs to sign the statement and Declaration under Penalty of Perjury, if that is required. Owners of businesses must bring suit for themselves and personally sign the declaration. Partnerships generally must sue under their business name, and any of the partners can sign the statement and the declaration. Some states allow unincorporated businesses to send an employee to represent the business in both filing the papers and appearing in court.

Corporations should sue under their own names, with a corporate officer or someone appointed by the officers signing the statement and declaration on the corporation's behalf. Any appointed representative of a corporation should carry a signed statement of authorization. In Illinois, Minnesota, New Mexico and the District of Columbia the corporation's representative must also be an attorney. New York, Pennsylvania and Rhode Island also require corporate representatives to be lawyers unless the corporation is a small business with limited assets. Ohio corporations need to be represented by attorneys unless they do not plan to argue the case or cross-examine witnesses.

Giving small-business owners a forum in which to settle minor disputes was one of the original goals of the small claims court system. Critics now contend that the courts are becoming glorified collection agencies in states where businesses are not barred from suing, or where no limit is placed on how often they may bring suit. Court policies vary regarding business plaintiffs, usually reflecting the court's own philosophy about how it should be used. For example, many states specifically prohibit "assignees" (third parties, usually collection agencies) from bringing suit to collect a bill on behalf of someone else. Also, many states limit the number of times anyone can bring suit within a given year—a further check on the use of the court for frequent debt collections.

Check Appendix I and ask the court clerk about any limitations on business plaintiffs.

In general, the person or business that has had a loss must bring suit. If, for example, the small claims suit is for damages to a car involved in a collision, the registered owner or owners of the car must file the suit. The driver, however, will probably be needed to testify in court.

In some restricted circumstances, rules expressly authorize third parties to bring suit on behalf of those injured. For example, minors are not allowed to sue but may get their claim into court by having a parent or legal guardian appointed as *guardian ad litem* to file suit on their behalf. Further, if a plaintiff is bedridden or severely disabled, judges in most states can appoint a friend or relative of the plaintiff as legal representative to file the small claims suit.

WHEN SHOULD YOU SUE?

For every type of small claims dispute (personal injury, property damage, contracts, and so on) your state's law specifies a time limit within which you must file suit. These limits (known as "statutes of limitations") are rarely less than one year and usually from one to five years.

If the original incident in your dispute occurred well over a year ago, you should check the statute of limitations in your state. The court clerk might know if your case has passed the deadline. If he or she does not, try a local law library. Your state's laws will be collected in a book called *Annotated Codes, Compiled Statutes* or something similar (the title is included at the head of each state's listing in Appendix I) and the information you need will probably be indexed under "Limitations of Actions." If you need help, ask the librarian.

If you are nearing the end of the statute of limitations, you may have another problem. The judge will want to know why you waited so long to file your suit. Your best answer is to show that you've been pursuing the complaint all along, reasonably and responsibly, and you were forced to turn to the court only because the statute of limitations was running out.

Remember that if the person you're suing was acting as an employee of a governmental agency, you must file and pursue a claim with that agency before you can file suit in court. Also, the time limit for filing a claim with the agency's grievance system may be very severe—often as short as thirty days—and if you miss that deadline, you may be precluded from suing in court at all. Check with the agency immediately after any incident to learn if you are facing a deadline.

WHAT SHOULD YOU CLAIM?

Claim as much as you can justify, but never more than the upper dollar limit allowed by the court. Remember, the judge has the power to award you less than you request but cannot give you more than the court's dollar limit allows. Because judges are allowed to award a percentage of your claim, it usually pays to estimate your damages on the high side when the real value of an item is uncertain. Costs involved in bringing your case to court are a separate matter, and will be discussed later.

The dollar limit in each state is occasionally raised so inflation won't rule out the types of disputes the court was intended to handle. Always check with the clerk about the current dollar limit. If your claim is larger than the current limit and you still want to use the small claims court, you are permitted to reduce your claim to fit within its limit. But if you do so, you are taking an irreversible legal step. Once you file a complaint on a particular matter for a stated sum, you automatically "waive the difference" and cannot claim more later. (See Appendix I for the limit in your area.)

In many cases, that makes sense because the cost of hiring a lawyer to represent you in formal court would be more than you would win. Say you have a $2,000 claim in a district that allows small claims cases up to only $1,500. Talk to local attorneys about their fees. If you can't find a lawyer who will take your case for $200 or less (including all legal fees and miscellaneous costs) and you believe you could represent yourself successfully in small claims court, you'll probably be better off there. But remember: you should feel confident that you can handle the case yourself and can convince the judge to award you most or all of the $1,500 limit allowed. To decide whether to go into small claims court on your own or into formal court with a lawyer, weigh carefully the strengths of your case and the costs involved. Then consider how you feel about the lawyers you interviewed, the amount they charge and whether you yourself have the time to prepare carefully for small claims court.[1]

There is another way to alter your claim to fit within your state's dollar limits: split it into two or more separate actions. In the case of Mrs. Jones and the roofers in Chapter 1, she could try splitting her $2,000 claim into a $1,500 claim seeking a return of the money paid for the "repairs," and a $500 claim for the water damage to her home.

If you plan to take this route, be sure your claim can be split into logically distinct parts. Issues that might appear separable to you may not be so in the eyes of the law. The small claims clerk may be willing to give you an opinion, but only the judge can decide whether you truly have two distinct claims. If you can build a defensible case for each, the judge will allow them and rule on each claim separately. If not, the judge will reject them and ask you to reduce the total amount to the court's limit, thereby waiving the difference, or take your case to a higher court. Be

---

[1]Before interviewing or hiring a lawyer, consult *Using a Lawyer,* by Kay Ostberg in association with HALT, Random House, 1990.

prepared to make this decision and to accept whatever the judge decides.

Once you're clear about the upper dollar limit, you must still compute your claim according to two primary rules: you are entitled only to damages that you've actually suffered; and you must be able to prove them.

Property Damage   When you sue for something that has been destroyed, you cannot recover what it cost, only what it was worth. For example, automobiles are valued by looking up advertisements for comparable models, and using the estimates in the "blue book" *(National Auto Dealers' Association Official Used Car Guide)*. If the car is only damaged and you produce repair estimates for less than the official value of the car, you can recover what it will cost to fix it.

However, beware: your car's total worth may be less than it would cost to fix it. In that case, whether or not it looks it to you, your car is a "total loss." You will be able to claim only the car's book value, minus what the car is worth as junk—"salvage value." Unless you can produce repair receipts to show that recent improvements make your car worth more than the standard book value, you'll probably be limited by this general formula.

Proving the value of other property is less formal and sometimes more difficult. Generally, you will have to prove what the item cost originally and to estimate how much of its useful life had been used when the damage occurred. With appliances and nonpersonal items, the court may resort to standard tables of depreciation, but when your wardrobe is marred, ruined or lost, judges are usually more willing to listen to claims about its personal value. Judges realize that damaged clothing must usually be replaced rather than repaired. If the clothing was relatively new, try to claim its original cost. If it was older, you can ask for slightly less than the original price, but expect the judge to reduce it somewhat.

Personal Injury   Personal injury cases that involve medical bills generally exceed small claims court limits. Minor injuries, however, are often part of small claims suits. When you calculate injury claims, remember that judges do not like to duplicate insurance benefits. You will be expected to prove all the expense you claim and to verify that none of them were covered by insurance or other benefits programs. These expenses may include transportation to the doctor's office and loss of wages, but you'll have to show that any wage loss caused by your injury wasn't compensated for as sick leave.

You can also claim compensation for the "pain and suffering" caused by your injury. Judges generally will accept this sort of claim only if it is accompanied by medical evidence of injury (such as medical bills or a statement from your doctor), plus a sincere account from you of the discomfort caused. It's always difficult to place a dollar value on misery. The easiest way is to subtract the total expenses you are claiming from the dollar limit allowed in court, then claim the difference for your pain and suffering. For example, in a personal injury case where you claim $2,000 in medical bills not covered by your insurance company and the court's dollar limit is $2,500, you could claim the remaining $500 for pain and suffering.

Contracts   Contract cases tend to be easier to determine because the amount in question is usually specified in the contract. If interest payments were mentioned in the contract, you'll have to compute the total interest due and specifically request it in the Plaintiff's Statement as part of your claim. If interest wasn't mentioned, you may want to try to claim it anyway.

Landlord-Tenant   Some states have created special penalties for landlords who unjustly fail to return cleaning or security deposits. In California, it is $200 plus the deposit. In Illinois, Michigan, New Jersey, Pennsylvania and several other states, it is double the deposit plus, sometimes, attorneys' fees. In Colorado, Georgia, Hawaii, Maryland, North Dakota, Texas and the District of Columbia it is triple the deposit. Texas is the toughest: it allows a claim of $100 plus three times the deposit, plus attorneys' fees. Since the judge may reduce your claim in court, you should always claim the maximum allowed. If you're a tenant planning to sue a landlord, you should ask the court what, if any, penalties are allowed in your state.

Some states that allow only cash awards also allow judges to issue eviction notices. Others have a separate landlord-tenant court. Still others will consider eviction only when the amount of rent due is less than the court's dollar limit. If your state allows eviction, a landlord may ask for it rather than a cash judgment.

Equitable Relief   If you live in a state that allows non-cash relief, you must place a dollar value on the cause of the dispute, then request a specific remedy. For example: "The market value of the vase was $500, but since it is irreplaceable I would like to request that it be ordered returned to me." Remember, it is entirely up to the judge to decide whether you receive the money or your specific request.

Other Costs   You can collect any costs you had to pay to bring the case to trial, such as filing fees and the costs of legal services. Because you won't know the total amount of "costs" at such an early stage, you can in your original claim state that you are claiming "$——— plus costs." Later, in the courtroom, you can request the actual amount you have spent.

WHY ARE YOU SUING?

You will notice that the space in the Plaintiff's Statement where you must state your complaint is minimal—usually no more than two or three lines. You are not pleading your case here, nor should you try to anticipate your opponent's objections. State the central facts only: indicate the type of dispute and perhaps the basic reason the defendant is to blame. For example: "Hottin Roofers failed to adequately repair the roof of my house and, as a result, substantial water damage occurred."

WHEN IS THE HEARING?

When you've completed the Plaintiff's Statement, set a date for the court hearing. In some states it is required that the hearing be held within a certain number of days from the date of filing. Others are less specific, but you can usually count on getting a hearing within four weeks.

The clerk will suggest a court date. You should accept it only if it seems convenient and gives you enough time to serve the defendant properly (see page 52). Give yourself at least a couple of weeks to make sure that the defendant is properly served with notice of your suit. If your case depends on the word of a witness, be sure to pick a day when you know your witness can appear. If it suits you better, ask the clerk if evening or Saturday sessions are available.

Recognize, too, that a court hearing set for 9 A.M. may not reach the judge until 3 P.M. Always get a good idea of how long the hearing *could* take before committing yourself to a particular day. It is an unfortunate fact that most small claims courts don't set an order for hearing cases until the morning of the appointed day.

You must be there for the roll call, even if it means waiting several hours to appear before a judge. Ask the clerk what hours the court is in session. If it's 9:00 to 5:00, plan to be there all day. If it's 9:00 to 12:00, you should be free by lunchtime.

If you have trouble serving notice on your opponent, you

can call the clerk and ask that the hearing date be post-poned. If you've served your opponent and then either side cannot make the hearing because of a scheduling conflict, you can have the date changed either with a letter to the clerk signed by both sides asking for a new date, or with a formal letter to the judge from either side explaining why a later date is necessary. In either letter, be sure to indicate clearly your case number (which will have been stamped on the Plaintiff's Statement by the clerk). Always send a copy of your letter to the judge and to your opponent.

WHAT ELSE IS NEEDED?

If you have specific questions about filing your claim, don't hesitate to ask the clerk. One of the clerk's primary duties is to make sure all filings are technically complete. Determine what your state requires and ask the clerk to look over your Plaintiff's Statement to see that it is correct. Some courts require certain documents as evidence (copies of contracts, bills, receipts, and so on), that must be submitted with the filing. The clerk will tell you what you need. Just be sure to bring *copies* of all relevant documents. Always keep the originals in your file.

The clerk will also ask you how you intend to serve the papers that notify the defendant you are suing. The various methods of "serving papers" are discussed in the following chapters.

CHAPTER 5

SERVING NOTICE

Once you've completed the Plaintiff's Statement and paid the filing fee, you must see that copies of the statement and other documents are properly delivered to the person you're suing. That person has a right to be informed fully of the claims, and to be given enough time to prepare a defense. The process of delivering the Plaintiff's Statement and other materials is called "serving the papers."

Each state has a specific sequence of procedures you must follow to serve your papers properly. The burden is on you to follow your state's rules exactly. If you do this, the court accepts that the other side has been notified and summoned to appear in defense. If the defendant then fails to appear in court in spite of the notice, you automatically win your case.

This victory is called a *default judgment.* The judge may ask you to state your case briefly to make sure the defendant was liable and that you haven't claimed too much, but you can be reasonably sure of being awarded most of your claim by default. In 1978 researchers John C. Ruhnka and Steven Weller published a valuable and unique two-year study that examined 7,218 cases from 15 small claims courts across the U.S.[1]

Ruhnka and Weller found that 44 percent of the cases

[1] *Small Claims Courts: A National Examination,* published by the National Center for State Courts, 1978.

ended in default. Because you stand a chance of winning your case by default, it's imperative that you do not ruin it because of improper service.

Some general rules about serving papers apply almost everywhere:

- You must serve the defendant a specified number of days before the trial, not counting the day of service or the day of trial.
- All defendants must be served individually, *even if they are married to each other.*
- You can serve someone who is in active military service, but no default judgment will be entered if that person fails to appear.
- In most states, although you can name a corporation as a defendant, you are required to serve one of its officers; some states, however, do allow you to serve an employee at the place of business.
- Out-of-state corporations may be required to have an in-state "registered agent" whom you can serve. If so, the office of the secretary of state in your state keeps these names and addresses on file. A registered agent is a person authorized to act on the company's behalf.

METHODS OF SERVICE

You can serve your papers in several different ways: by mail, in person and by "substituted service." States' rules vary about which method is preferred. Ask the court clerk about the preferred order of service in your jurisdiction.

It is almost always acceptable to have a law officer serve your papers, although they are permitted to do so only within their jurisdiction and generally charge a fee. The charge for service by a sheriff or marshal ranges from $2 to $15. A professional process server can also be hired for about $20. Some states even permit service by a court-approved "disinterested adult"—anyone of legal age who is not a party to the suit.

In most states, mailing the papers by registered or certified mail and getting a return receipt signed by the person you're suing will prove you served the papers and when. Some states require that this method be tried first. Generally, the clerk does the mailing and you pay postage and handling costs when you file your suit. Some states require that the papers be served within the small claims district where you file your suit. This can cause you a problem if you and the defendant live and work in different districts. In this situation, you are virtually forced to file suit in the defendant's small claims district, not yours—the one instance in which you might be forced to file suit where it is inconvenient for you.

WHAT CAN GO WRONG?

States that allow or require certified or registered mail will want a signed receipt by the defendant as proof of service. Because the court clerk handles this in most states, you'll have to call the clerk's office to find out if the signed receipt has arrived. The problem with service by mail is that some mail carriers will let anyone at the correct address sign for the letter. It is *not* a valid service if the defendant does not sign or, in some states, if he or she personally refuses to accept the letter. When you call the clerk to ask if the delivery has been recorded, always ask if the defendant's name is the one signed on the receipt.

If service by registered or certified mail fails, you must go on to the next step, probably in-person service. This means the Plaintiff's Statement and other documents must be handed personally to the defendant, but not by you. You can't personally serve the defendant, but if your state permits personal service by a disinterested adult, you can save the process server's fee by asking a friend or relative to do it for you. Usually, the server need only be an adult resident of the state. You can hire a law officer or professional process server, of course, but this will increase the cost of bringing your case to trial, an expense that might not be reimbursed if you lose the case, if the judge decides against awarding costs or if you have a problem with collecting your award.

For personal service, you'll need a packet of forms from the court known as a "Declaration and Order." The server signs part of this (the "Proof of Service" form) and returns it to the court. This verifies that service was accomplished. If the defendant later claims that the papers were never served, the court will ask the server who signed the form to testify whether the service was performed or not.

If you are concerned about an evasive or abusive defendant or dangerous neighborhoods, law officers or professional servers should be used. Law officers' fees usually are less expensive and most people are intimidated enough by the authority of a sheriff or marshal to accept the papers. If the person you're suing refuses to accept the forms, the server, whether a law officer or disinterested adult, should simply state what the papers are—a notice of a lawsuit in small claims court—and leave them there. For most courts, testimony from the server that papers were delivered is enough.

Beyond these general rules, each state's requirements for proper service are different. Some of these procedures are relaxed or otherwise changed, when you are suing a business. You can get a basic idea of what your state requires by checking Appendix I, but the final word must come from the clerk of the court in which you file suit. Don't hesitate to ask for advice about the preferred or required methods of service.

CHAPTER 6

IF YOU'RE SUED

If you are being sued (the defendant), you will prepare for trial in almost the same way as the person suing you. The only significant difference is that you will not have to file a Plaintiff's Statement. To seek alternative resolution procedures, to collect evidence, to prepare for trial and so on, simply use this book as a plaintiff would.

If you know how a plaintiff goes about proving loss and liability, it will not be too difficult to make basic decisions about your defense. Essentially, you must weigh the merits of the case against you and decide between defending yourself and paying the claim.

FILING AN ANSWER

In some states, if you intend to defend yourself, you must file a "responsive pleading" (generally called an "Answer") to the Plaintiff's Statement *before* the trial. This simple form requires you to state whether you intend to contest the claim and if so, to state the basis of your objection to it. You may deny liability completely or merely object to the size of the plaintiff's claim. The majority of states do not require you to file anything—all you need to do is show up on the day of your trial.

While one state, South Carolina, allows an oral response, it encourages defendants to submit written responses. If you insist on giving an oral one, it must be given directly to the judge. The important thing is to give your Answer, whether oral or written, to the appropriate person (clerk or judge) within the required number of days before trial. (Be sure to ask if weekends or holidays are counted.) If you fail to meet this deadline, you may be subject to an automatic default.

If you must answer in writing, always call the clerk to make sure your Answer was received on time. Be sure to ask if evidence supporting your defense, such as bills and receipts, must also be filed before the hearing. If you've missed the deadline for filing an Answer because of late or improper service, or because of extenuating circumstances, ask the clerk about filing a "Motion to Vacate Judgment" (see Chapter 9).

DEFENDING YOURSELF

You can construct a solid defense for yourself in one of three ways: by arguing that the amount of money being claimed is greatly exaggerated; by denying you're the one to blame for the loss; or by denying you're to blame and filing a counterclaim against the person suing you.

Challenging the Amount When you contest only the size of the plaintiff's claim, you will be admitting at least partial responsibility. You will argue either that you are not entirely responsible for the total damage, or that the damage was not as great as the plaintiff claims. You may try to argue both points.

Denying full responsibility means you'll have to prove the plaintiff was partly responsible for the damage. In the example of Mrs. Jones and the roofers, this might mean proving that she allowed the water to sit for days, compounding the damage. Denying an inflated dollar claim, on the other hand, means proving that the plaintiff's evidence of loss is either insufficient or incorrect. In either case, collect and present your counterevidence exactly as you would if you were the one suing.

Denying Liability   You may be able to deny all liability. If you are in no way responsible for any loss suffered by the plaintiff, collect the evidence required to prove it. (The way both plaintiffs and defendants collect and present evidence is discussed in Chapter 8.)

"Technical" defenses can also be used against liability. For example, the statute of limitations may have expired. If the case involves the sale of a product or service, state or federal consumer protection statutes might protect you completely. You may, however, need legal advice to unearth such defense strategies (see Chapter 7).

If you were not served notice of the suit in the required way, as described in Chapter 3, that fact alone is not a valid defense. At best, it is a good reason to ask for a continuance or Motion to Vacate Judgment (see Chapter 9). Even if you know that the service of the Plaintiff's Statement was technically invalid, do not fail to show up at the trial. If you are not there, you will probably lose by default.

Counterclaims   You may want both to deny you're at fault and to file a counterclaim for damages you suffered because of the original incident. If, for example, you are being sued because you failed to pay for the rental of an automobile tow bar, you may want to countersue, claiming that the bar was so poorly made it damaged the car you towed with it. This is one of those cases in which the other side beat you to court even though you had better grounds to sue. Many unscrupulous people believe that the best defense is a good offense. Don't be taken in: you have the right to sue even while you are being sued.

Remember that filing a counterclaim is just like filing an independent suit: you must establish loss and liability. In the tow bar example, proving that the equipment rented was worthless exempts you only from fulfilling the rental contract: you won't have to pay the rental fee. To have a valid counterclaim, you must also prove you suffered a further loss—the damage to your car—because of the defective equipment.

To file a counterclaim, prepare a "Claim of Defendant." In some states you must do this before the trial on the original suit. Completing this form is exactly like filing a Plaintiff's Statement, and, like the plaintiff, you must pay a fee. In a few states you may wait and counterclaim at the trial, but this has little "surprise" value because the person suing you will probably request and be given a continuance to collect further evidence.

Be careful about counterclaiming in excess of the small claims court's dollar limits. If you do so, in most states it will automatically transfer your case to a higher court. The amount of money involved may be enough that you want to go to formal court and accept the higher costs involved, but this should be avoided if possible. New York, North Carolina, Vermont and Washington do not even allow counterclaims that exceed the court's dollar limits. In other words, in those states, your case will not automatically be transferred; you'll have to file a separate lawsuit in the higher court. For more information on counterclaims, see Appendix I.

You might also consider a cross-claim. This is a suit brought by you as one defendant against a *codefendant,* asking for full or partial relief if that person was responsible for the damage that led to the suit against you. For example, if your landlord sues you and your roommate for nonpayment of rent, you could file a cross-claim against your roommate to recover money you already paid her to help meet the rent payments.

OTHER OPTIONS

Jury Trials　Small claims are almost never decided by a jury, though in a few states the defendant can ask for a jury trial. Usually this means your case is transferred to a higher court, but a few states do offer small claims jury trials. These trials take longer to schedule, and you may have to post a bond or pay a fee to cover the added cost. This almost always makes requesting a small claims jury trial a waste of time and money.

Transfers　Some states allow a defendant to ask for a transfer to a higher court without either counterclaiming or requesting a jury. Because a defendant who loses may be forced to pay the plaintiff's court costs, this is an extremely unwise maneuver, especially as court costs are much higher in upper civil courts than in small claims court. For more information on jury trials and transfers, see Appendix I.

SETTLING OUT OF COURT

If you know you're liable for the loss and the dollar claim is reasonably accurate, the best defense is to cut your losses: offer to settle out of court for an amount less than what the plaintiff is asking.

Plaintiffs usually overestimate their losses because they expect the judge to reduce their claim. If that's the case, try urging the person suing you to settle for less and to save the irritation and time that could be spent collecting evidence and sitting in court.

As discussed in Chapter 9, most plaintiffs settle for about 75 percent of their original claim. Knowing this, defendants usually offer about 50 percent and then negotiate upward to a mutually acceptable figure.

If you and the person suing you can agree on a settlement figure, you may also be able to work out a plan of installment payments. This will reduce your immediate financial burden and help assure the plaintiff of eventually receiving payment. If you can't agree on an amount or a payment schedule before trial, you'll have to decide between arbitration and a court hearing. Chapters 2 and 9 discuss these options.

AFTER THE JUDGMENT

If you are sued in small claims court and lose, you have an option not available in other courts: you can ask the judge to order installment payments, allowing you to distribute your payments over a long period of time. This method prevents the person who sued you from garnishing your wages. It also means your personal property won't be seized as long as you meet the payment schedule.

Such installment payments are an alternative in almost every small claims district, but not all judges will order them. Ask the court clerk if your judge allows installment payments. If he or she does not, ask for a continuance or postponement and hope for a more enlightened judge. For more information on installment payments, see Chapter 10.

CHAPTER 7

LEGAL
HELP

You must decide if you want to be represented in court by a lawyer. If you did not have trouble completing the Plaintiff's Statement or the Answer, it's highly unlikely you will need a lawyer's services. Private lawyers are not, of course, the only source of legal help, and we will discuss less expensive alternatives.

Before making a decision about using a lawyer, check your state's small claims rules. Some states prohibit the use of lawyers in small claims courts; a few require corporations to be represented by a lawyer; others permit both the plaintiff and the defendant to bring a lawyer to court. The use of a lawyer by both sides in a few of these states will, however, mean that the case is transferred to regular civil court. For your state's rules, see Appendix I.

DO YOU NEED A LAWYER?

Ruhnka and Weller, whom we discussed earlier, discovered in their 1978 survey that plaintiffs who used lawyers won just as often as those who did not—when going up against defendants without a lawyer. The researchers also found that when plaintiffs hired or consulted a lawyer, judges awarded them less of what they had sued for than they awarded plaintiffs who did not use a lawyer.

It is especially interesting to note that plaintiffs in the lowest educational and income groups received considerably higher awards when they were *not* represented by a lawyer. Ruhnka and Weller suggest that better-educated plaintiffs were able to select better lawyers, but a more likely explanation is that judges, who are normally predisposed to protect plaintiffs, are even more likely to do so when they think the plaintiff is not sophisticated.

The story *appears* to be different for defendants. Defendants *with* lawyers won more often when facing unrepresented plaintiffs than defendants without lawyers. And defendants with lawyers always did better in reducing the claim against them, whether the plaintiff did or did not have a lawyer.

The statistics, however, don't give the whole picture. Ruhnka and Weller note that plaintiffs generally have more time to collect evidence and have more information and help in preparing for trial. If nothing else, plaintiffs can learn a lot from a clerk while preparing their initial Plaintiff's Statement. Most defendants, on the other hand, don't prepare for court and simply show up on the day of the trial. Further, they aren't given the basic information in the court's brochure when they are served with the Plaintiff's Statement. It should not be surprising, then, that defendants with lawyers are better prepared and therefore more likely to win.

Lawyers can be particularly helpful to defendants in consumer cases. The failure of a manufacturer or creditor to observe state or federal consumer protection laws is usually a complete defense against liability for what you might owe that manufacturer or creditor. For example, the Fair Credit Billing Act says that you may stop payment for any poor-quality goods or services purchased with a credit card if you have made a genuine attempt to solve the problem, as discussed in Chapters 1 and 2. To qualify, however, the purchases must have been made within the same state as, or within 100 miles of, the cardholder's billing address.

Ruhnka and Weller also found that most judges they interviewed knew little or nothing about federal regulations such as the Consumer Product Safety Act, Consumer Credit Protection Act, Fair Interest Labeling Act, the Magnuson-Moss Warranty Act, or even state provisions such as the Uniform Consumer Credit Code (UCCC). This should not be surprising as most consumer cases do not involve enough money to be taken to formal court, where judges are more apt to deal with and be informed about new laws.

THE VERDICT ON LAWYERS

It's worth noting that plaintiffs and defendants, both winners and losers, who used lawyers were less satisfied with their small claims experience than those who had not. Ruhnka and Weller believe this is "possibly because the additional cost of a lawyer reduced their recovery or added to their loss." It's easy to agree with this assessment.

Here are some guidelines for whether you, as a plaintiff or defendant, should hire an attorney to handle or help you with a small claims suit:

If you are a plaintiff and don't have difficulty understanding this book or filing the Plaintiff's Statement, it is unlikely you will need a lawyer. This is true even if the other side is represented by one. If you have a lawyer in this situation, it could reduce the size of your recovery, push the matter into a higher court and perhaps lose the judge as an ally.

A judge's willingness to help an unrepresented person is perhaps the best argument for appearing without a lawyer in court. Judges recognize that nonlawyers are at a technical disadvantage when facing a lawyer in the courtroom, and most judges try to correct the imbalance. As one judge told Ruhnka and Weller: "When one side is without a lawyer, the natural tendency of a judge is to favor the underdog—and when the judge is acting as lawyer for one side, as well as the judge, you can imagine that the judge's client will not lose too often."

If you are a defendant, legal advice can be important, but having a lawyer in court may be both counterproductive and expensive. What's important is that unrepresented defendants tend to lose, not because they don't have a lawyer, but because they do not have adequate information and are unprepared for court. You don't have to hire a lawyer to seek specific legal advice or to prepare your case. Less expensive and better alternatives are available, as we will see.

SEEKING LEGAL ADVICE

Even if your small claims court prohibits the use of a lawyer in court, nothing stops you from seeking legal advice beforehand. The particulars of your case may lead to legal questions about such matters as liability, court limitations and consumer protection laws. Still, you needn't pay a lawyer a lot of money to get the answers.

Some small claims courts (in California, Chicago, New York City and Washington, D.C., for example) have law students, advisors or paralegals in the courthouse to answer questions and help you prepare the necessary papers. Also, many law schools operate clinics that help people answer basic legal questions. Ask the court clerk if this sort of help is available in your area.

Next, try a private or governmental consumer action agency if your case involves a purchase of any kind. These agencies have staff lawyers and paralegals knowledgeable about consumer protection and other laws that govern commercial transactions. If you do need a lawyer with whom to discuss your consumer case, the private agencies will probably be able to recommend someone.

Other sources of free legal advice are also available. If you are having a problem with a creditor, for example, talk with the lawyer at your bank. Other questions might be resolved in a brief meeting with a staff lawyer in the company where you work.

If you do need to consult a private attorney, you'll want to keep the cost as low as possible. When you make an appointment, be sure to say you want to seek legal advice, not representation in court. If you have your materials properly prepared, you could be out of the lawyer's office in a half hour—getting all the advice you need for a relatively small sum. [1]

[1]For more information on cutting the costs of legal help, see *Using a Lawyer* by Kay Ostberg in association with HALT, Random House, 1990.

CHAPTER 8

PREPARING FOR TRIAL

You must do two things to prepare your case for trial: collect the evidence and plan your presentation. If you are the one who is suing, you can begin even before you leave the clerk's office. If you are being sued, you should probably go to the clerk's office even if you don't have to file an Answer to the Plaintiff's Statement.

Ask the clerk if the small claims court is currently in session and get directions to the courtroom being used. Also ask the clerk if the judge who is presiding will be presiding on the scheduled trial date. This is unlikely. Judges usually preside in small claims courts only for a specified period and then rotate back to higher courts. If the present judge will not cover your case, ask the clerk when the rotation occurs. You may want to return before your trial and watch your judge in action.

In any event, it's wise to visit the courtroom. As you will see, the only significant difference between a typical small claims court and a formal trial court is that usually the courtroom has no witness stand and no jury. The judge sits at a raised bench, a clerk sits at a small table before the bench, and they are faced by a long table or tables for the plaintiff, defendant and witnesses. A railing behind the plaintiff and defendant separates the participants from seats provided for the public.

If a hearing is in progress, take a seat at the back and

watch the proceedings. A few minutes of your time will demonstrate the two essential elements of a small claims trial: it is extremely short and the judge is completely in control.

Most small claims trials last no more than twenty minutes. This means you probably will have about five minutes to present your case. If you are disorganized and fail to get essential information to the judge in this amount of time, you may well lose. Judges tend to be sympathetic to plaintiffs. They know you probably wouldn't have gone to the trouble to come to court unless you honestly believed you had been wronged. However, a small claims court is a busy place and dozens of other people will be waiting to have their cases heard. If you can't make your case in a few minutes, the judge will simply have to make a decision based on whatever you have managed to get across.

This brings up the second essential point, the role of the judge. All judges apply the law's standards to the facts *as presented*. They then reach a decision that establishes responsibility and the extent of damage. How they manage to arrive at that decision varies considerably.

Some small claims judges are "active," while others are more passive. The activist judge conducts court like an investigation. Based on the Plaintiff's Statement and supporting materials such as your two letters, the judge will quickly decide what the legal essentials are and begin questioning both sides in an attempt to get to the heart of the matter. Judges who use this approach do so to move the trial along. They do not want to listen to either side ramble on about unessential matters.

Passive judges behave more as they do in higher courts. They sit back, listen to both sides tell their story, then make a decision. If either side wants to ramble and fails to make a case, so be it. The judge sees the judicial role as that of an aloof, impartial arbiter of the facts presented.

Ruhnka and Weller's examination of small claims courts across the country found the number of active and passive judges to be about equal—even within individual districts. You may have to appear before either type, so be prepared for both. Whichever sort of judge you are assigned, the preparation is the same with respect to gathering your evidence. The real difference occurs in the presentation of that evidence. The activist judge will expect you to have it ready when he or she asks for it. The passive judge will expect you to present it to him or her in a coherent order of your own choosing.

COLLECTING EVIDENCE

Ruhnka and Weller also asked judges what aspect of small claims cases caused them the most trouble. Most said difficulties almost always resulted from unclear recitation of facts and damages. In such cases, neither side offered a "preponderance of evidence."

The preponderance-of-evidence rule is legal jargon that simply means that it's up to the plaintiff to present more evidence to support a claim than the defendant can present to challenge it. In other words, at least 51 percent of the facts must favor the plaintiff for the case to succeed. Judges often compare this rule to a set of balance scales. The plaintiff and defendant each puts all of the available evidence on opposite sides of the scale. If the plaintiff's side is heavier, the plaintiff wins. If the defendant's side is heavier—or if the scale seems level—the defendant wins.

The preponderance-of-evidence rule applies in formal civil courts as well as in small claims courts. Some small claims judges, however, relax the rule somewhat. If the evidence for both sides is roughly equal, they tend to favor the plaintiff. Passive judges are usually more strict about the rules of evidence, but even they tend to sympathize with plaintiffs.

Nevertheless, no judge will decide for a plaintiff if the

defendant clearly is supported by most of the evidence. It's up to you to collect and organize every available piece of evidence or risk the consequences.

The evidence you need depends on your case, but whatever the case, certain rules will apply. All you need to know about the rules in small claims court is that small claims judges will rate evidence in the following order of importance:

- Documentary evidence
- Expert testimony
- Witnesses
- Your testimony and opinion

As you can see, your testimony and opening remarks are of less importance than hard documentary evidence. If your presentation amounts to nothing more than telling your story to the judge and the other side shows up with hard evidence or witnesses, be prepared to lose.

Documentary Evidence

Documentary evidence is not hard to collect. It consists of your two earlier letters demanding restitution for your losses plus receipts, canceled checks, police reports, photographs and other physical evidence. If you've followed the instructions in Chapter 1, most of the documents you'll need are already in your file. The two complaint letters are especially important. They demonstrate that you behaved responsibly throughout and, more important, they set the agenda for the trial. They briefly summarize what happened, how much money was involved and why the person you're suing is liable. They will focus attention on these specific points and force the judge to see why your evidence is relevant and conclusive.

The letters do not "prove" the essential points of your case. They only help you determine what other documents are needed. You will need further evidence to establish loss and liability.

Evidence of Loss   Before you filed your Plaintiff's Statement you determined the amount you lost. The supporting evidence you'll need includes any document that justifies the amount you're claiming. All relevant repair bills, estimates, receipts, contracts, canceled checks and the like are essential.

If you can bring the damaged item into court (such as a coat damaged by the cleaners), by all means do so. If that is not possible, bring photographs, if they clearly show the amount of damage. A photo of your water-damaged wallpaper, for example, can be very convincing.

Some small claims courts have their own rules of evidence for proving damages. Many, for example, require three independent repair estimates to establish a claim in an auto accident case. Be sure to ask the clerk if any such special requirements apply to your case.

Evidence of Liability   Documentary evidence that establishes liability is harder to collect. For example, if you were in an auto accident and a police report was filed, neither that report nor a traffic ticket issued at the scene automatically establishes liability, although both may support your contention.

If a written contract is involved, liability may be a little easier to establish. Be sure to bring a copy of the contract to court with you: it contains the other side's promise to do something. In contract cases, you only have to concentrate on showing how that promise was broken.

Beyond that, proving liability can call for some creative thinking on your part. An expert witness may be the solution. In other situations, look for a visual aid to demonstrate the problem to the judge. Judges often have difficulty reaching a decision because it's difficult to visualize what's in dispute. For instance, you could diagram on posterboard the intersection where the auto accident occurred to show exactly what happened. If your dispute involves the faulty installation of a pneumatic compressor, you'd better find a way to simply and clearly demonstrate what a compressor is and what it is supposed to do. Remember: most judges know little or nothing about electronics or complex machinery, and you will have less than five minutes in which to explain it.

Expert Testimony

Because judges cannot make on-site inspections of damage and often know little about the subject matter in dispute, you may need the help of an expert witness—someone who is qualified to report on the damage or liability and who is not involved with either side. You may want such witnesses to be present or to supply you with an affidavit.

Consider, for example, a dispute involving an appliance store's failure to repair or replace your defective TV set. If you drag the set into court, the judge won't be able to decide anything just by looking at it and the store's technician will probably blame your troubles on your misuse of the set. Who will the judge believe—you or a professional? However much the judge may want to believe you, you'll have to help. The best method is to have an independent technician look at the set and either come to court or sign an affidavit declaring under oath that the flaw is in the set.

For repair or installation problems, it's always wise to secure expert testimony. The problem is both getting it and getting it to court. Service representatives will probably charge you for an estimate, and few will want to spend an afternoon sitting in court.

However, if you have followed the advice in this book, you may have some of this evidence already in hand. If you tried to resolve your problem through a Better Business Bureau, Consumer Action Panel, consumer action agency or trade association, for example, one or more of those agencies probably sent an expert to check your claim. You might be able to use this expert's testimony at no charge. If this hasn't happened yet, these same agencies may provide or recommend an expert who will do this free or for a small fee. Testimony from an expert working with these associations should effectively demolish any technical bluffing from the other side.

Getting an expert to appear in person in court can be troublesome and costly and is usually unnecessary, at least in small claims court. A notarized letter to the court on business stationery describing the problem, its origin and the extent of the damage is probably enough. Always check with the court clerk to make sure that a signed and perhaps notarized letter is acceptable.

It is *always* a good idea for your expert witnesses to list telephone numbers where they can be reached on the day of the trial. Many judges will call from the bench to clear up any objections raised by the other side. If it becomes abundantly clear during the trial that you need your expert in court, ask the judge to postpone the hearing until you can arrange an appearance (see "Continuances" on page 87).

Other Witnesses

At times you may need other witnesses to verify what happened—people who were involved in the events or who merely observed them. The best are those who are neither involved in the dispute nor related to you. Passers-by who witnessed the auto accident or dog attack are ideal. Friends and relatives can also testify on your behalf, but a judge is obliged to recognize that they may be prejudiced in your favor.

Any witness is better than none. This is particularly true in landlord-tenant cases when the landlord withholds a security deposit claiming you damaged the rental property. Without "before and after" photographs or a detailed itemization of conditions when you moved in, it will be your word against the landlord's unless you have witnesses.

If you have friends or relatives who saw the place when you moved in and when you moved out, you should get their testimony. It will be particularly useful if your witness helped you clean the place when moving out. Judges understand that most landlords have an overly narrow definition of what constitutes normal wear and tear. What you need to establish, through a witness or through receipts, is that you made a reasonable effort to maintain the place properly.

It's important that you try to get your nonexpert witnesses to appear personally in court rather than sending a letter or sworn statement. A judge may believe the affidavit of an expert who has professional training and a need to preserve a professional reputation, but nonexpert witnesses' credibility depends largely on their behavior before the judge. If they seem rational and not excessively prejudiced, the judge is more likely to believe them.

If your witness absolutely cannot appear, you will have to settle for an affidavit. Be sure your witness explains in the affidavit why it is impossible to be in court; see that the witness's description of the incident is clear; and get a telephone number where the witness can be reached during the trial, if necessary.

Your Own Testimony

Your own testimony and opinion will be summarized in your first complaint letter. In court, the principal purpose of your testimony is to clarify any questions the judge has.

If you are facing an especially passive judge, your testimony may have to tie all of the evidence together, but your job is only to present the facts, not to establish their truth. Otherwise you'll be caught in a my-word-against-yours trap, and if the other side has evidence to support his or her version of the events, the preponderance of evidence will weigh against you. Present the best, hardest evidence you can find and let it speak for itself. Your job should be only to hand it to the judge and explain its relevance.

In negligence cases, you may be the only witness on your own behalf. In that case, your testimony is the evidence with regard to liability, but proving the amount of your loss will still require other evidence: receipts, canceled checks, bills and the like.

PLANNING YOUR PRESENTATION

Your role depends largely upon the sort of judge you're assigned. But whether you have to display your evidence in a logical order before a passive judge or simply wait for an active judge to ask for it, the evidence must still be ordered properly and readily available.

The most important thing is to weed out material that is not essential or relevant to the points you must prove. Prepare a folder or file for presentation to the judge. Include three sections: documents that give a chronological history of the dispute; documents that establish liability; and materials that prove the extent of your loss.

The first section needn't be more than your two letters of complaint and something to verify your attempts to seek out-of-court resolution—through the Better Business Bureau, a consumer action agency or arbitration. The second section should include relevant warranties, repair bills and affidavits from expert witnesses, if any. The third section should contain repair estimates, receipts and the like.

Put these materials in a logical order so the judge can see the history of the dispute at a glance. Don't expect the judge to read any more than the Plaintiff's Statement, perhaps your two letters, and a particular affidavit. Remember the constraints on the judge's time.

If you have any doubts about what may or may not be essential evidence, check with the consumer action agency or similar office you've dealt with before. Such groups have a lot of experience with small claims procedures. Keep your "marginal" evidence in a second file and be prepared to present it only if the judge asks for clarification on some point.

Your first folder's material will serve as your outline for a presentation if you face a passive judge. The verbal description of the incident and your attempts at resolution can be a simple recitation of the facts from your first letter and a description of facts supported by other evidence in the file.

A judge who wants to see other evidence—an expert's letter, for example—will ask for it. The important thing is to let the judge know you have it available. With any luck, even the passive judge will want to see your folder the first time you refer to it. Once you have presented your hard evidence, there's little if anything you should have to add.

If you think you'll be facing a passive judge, you might want to practice your presentation before a friend, neighbor or colleague, not as a form of amateur theatrics but to see if you can tell your story in five minutes or less and make sense of it to someone who knows none of its history. Your listener may have questions that never occurred to you. Those questions may even prompt you to collect further evidence.

GETTING EVIDENCE TO COURT

The evidence you will need for trial should be fairly easy to collect. However, special situations arise when knowing how to subpoena a witness or evidence can be useful. As you read the remainder of this chapter, remember that subpoenas are designed to resolve particular problems. They should never be used indiscriminately.

Subpoena of Witnesses

In most states, you can force a witness to appear in court by having a subpoena issued. Subpoena forms can be obtained from the clerk, and the process of serving the subpoena is like that of serving a Plaintiff's Statement. State rules vary but many require two things: that the witness you are subpoenaing live within a specified distance of the courthouse, and that the witness be entitled to collect a fee on demand when served the subpoena. The typical fee is $30 to $35, plus mileage.

Never force a witness who is unwilling to come and testify in your behalf. A witness who is angry about being dragged into court is unlikely to be very helpful before the judge and may even testify against you. If your witness needs a subpoena in order to take time off from work, arrange the court date in advance and get the witness's approval *before* you get the subpoena.

Make sure the witness's version of what happened is the version you want to have told in court. Nothing is wrong with coaching a witness about what part of the testimony is essential to your case. In fact, it is a good idea to rehearse with the witness to make sure that the testimony given will be favorable to you. Of course, you should never ask a witness to lie on your behalf. The penalty for this, if it should come to the court's attention, could be jail for both of you—you for obstructing justice and your witness for committing perjury. If you and your witness can't agree on what happened, *don't bring the witness to court.*

In some states, you can subpoena a police officer to appear if testimony is needed to supplement a vague police report. This can be expensive, however, because you usually have to pay a deposit equal to a day's wages for the officer and unless the appearance takes significantly less than a full day's time, you probably won't get any of it back. A more sensible alternative is to see if the officer has a "court day" scheduled during the month, then try to have your hearing scheduled for the same day.

In any event, it's seldom worth the expense to subpoena a police officer to appear in court. As with other expert witnesses, an affidavit will usually do. If it becomes clear the officer does need to be in court, the judge will postpone the hearing until a later date.

Subpoenas of Documents

You can subpoena documents just as you can witnesses. It's unusual in small claims court, but at times it may be necessary. For example, you may need copies of invoices, receipts, delivery records, or other documents to establish that a business transaction occurred.

To subpoena documents, ask the clerk for a form called a *subpoena duces tecum*—Latin for "under penalty you shall take it with you." It's much like the form for subpoenaing a witness, except it provides ample space for describing the documents you want. Always be specific about what documents you want brought to court. Give dates, invoice numbers, a description of the goods or services you bought, and so on. If you are not exact, the other side may show up with a 500-page computer printout no judge will take the time to look through.

You must attach to your subpoena a sworn statement explaining why the documents you want are essential in presenting your case. To save time, prepare the statement before you go to the clerk's office and bring extra copies. Sign it (and the copies, if necessary) in front of the clerk.

The clerk will help you complete the subpoena but, as with your Plaintiff's Statement, you must do some research before you go to the clerk's office. You'll have to know the name and address of whomever is directly in charge of the documents you are seeking. If you get the wrong person, your subpoena may be ignored. The safest bet is to name the person in charge of the correct department, the manager of the bookkeeping department, for example. You can get this person's name simply by calling the company or institution involved.

The person you name in the subpoena must be served

personally and, like subpoenaed witnesses, is entitled to a witness fee. That person will then be ordered to appear in court on the day of trial and to present the requested documents to the judge—not to you. If you need to see the documents, ask the judge if you can look them over while other cases are being tried.

Caution: a subpoena of documents, like a subpoena of witnesses, should be used only as a last resort. Never subpoena documents unless you are sure they are critical to your case and then only after all other efforts to get them have failed. A telephone call asking for photocopies may get you what you need. As with police officers and other expert witnesses, it's usually best to let the judge decide whether the original documents are required in court.

COLLECTING YOUR COSTS

It should be clear by now that subpoenaing expert witnesses, other witnesses and documents can be expensive. If you win, you can ask the judge to add these costs to your damage award. If the judge feels the subpoena was necessary, you'll probably get your money back. If, however, the judge believes you've needlessly wasted a day of a police officer's or anyone else's time, expect to have to pay a bill as high as $100.

That's why it's wise to let the judge decide if it is necessary to subpoena someone. If it becomes clear that an affidavit or a follow-up telephone call won't resolve important questions, the judge's willingness to grant a postponement signals that he or she at least believes a subpoena is necessary. This makes recovering your costs virtually a sure bet—if you win.

CHAPTER 9

BEFORE TRIAL

When you sue in a small claims court, you have a good chance of winning. As Ruhnka and Weller's study showed, almost half of all small claims defendants fail to show up for trial and thus lose by default, and when both sides do appear in court, 72 percent of the plaintiffs win.

If you're the one being sued, don't give up hope if you have good reasons for having the suit dismissed or the claim reduced. It's not difficult to win if you collect and present your evidence coherently.

For either side, the important things are: to know how the small claims system works; to be prepared; and to make the best possible presentation. If you've followed the advice in this book, your appearance in court should be something of an anticlimax. All you have to do at this point is follow a few basic rules.

YOUR ARRIVAL

The first and most basic rule is get to court on time. If, like most defendants, you haven't been to court before, or if you aren't sure which room the hearing is in, go early. The small claims session may begin with a roll call by the clerk, and if you're late, you may lose by default. Also, the option to appear before an arbitrator or mediator might be offered only at the beginning of the session.

Before the session begins, check the court calendar. This is a list of the cases to be heard that day. It is usually posted on a notice board outside the courtroom. If it is not, try the clerk's office. Sometimes only the clerk in the courtroom has a copy and your best opportunity to hear it is during the initial roll call.

Make sure your case is on the list. If it's not, ask the clerk why.

The next thing is to see if the calendar is divided into "case" and "motion" lists. If your case is on the "case" list, it will be heard during the session. If it's on the "motion" list, it means the other side has asked that the hearing be postponed. If the motion was made the same day as the trial so you couldn't have known of it even if you had called the clerk in advance, it's probably a delaying tactic and you should plan to fight it (see "Continuances," page 87.)

DEFAULTS

If you're the one bringing the suit and the other side (the defendant) fails to show up on the day of the trial, the judge will usually, as a matter of procedure, enter a default judgment against the defendant. That means you win.

On the other hand, if the defendant shows up for trial and you don't, one of several things can happen. The judge will either dismiss the case or decide it on the basis of the defendant's evidence, even though you're not there. If the judge does the latter, the case is settled once and for all. If, however, the judge dismisses the case, the plaintiff may, depending on the court rules of your particular state, get the chance to refile the claim against you. In most states the judge will dismiss the case "without prejudice," which means it will be taken off the calendar but can be refiled by the plaintiff at a later date. You can, however, ask the judge to dismiss the case "with prejudice." This prohibits the plaintiff from bringing the same suit against you again. Whether or not the judge can grant your request depends partly on how good a case you have and on what the court rules allow concerning defaults and dismissals.

If neither side shows up, the case is usually dismissed without prejudice, but in some states (Colorado and Texas, for example) the defendant automatically defaults.

In some courts the clerk can enter a default judgment if you have enough evidence to establish a simple claim (an unpaid bill, for example) but in most states you will have to appear before the judge, whether you're the one suing or the one being sued. The judge will ask a few simple questions, mostly to make sure that, if you're the plaintiff, you aren't claiming too much. Once assured, the judge will enter a judgment of default.

If you're the defendant, the judge will either dismiss the case or consider the merits of the claim against you on the basis of your evidence alone. A judge is more likely to enter a final decision on your case or to dismiss it with prejudice, if it is clear you are thoroughly prepared and if your witnesses took the trouble to show up.

Usually a default judgment doesn't go into effect until after a grace period of ten to sixty days. This gives the one who missed the hearing time to file a "Motion to Vacate Judgment." The motion asks the judge to erase the default and reschedule the case for a hearing. You can file it simply by asking the clerk's office for the proper form, filling it out and giving it to the clerk.

A judge is unlikely to grant such a motion unless you can establish one of two things: that an emergency made it impossible for you either to attend or to give the court notice by asking for your case to be rescheduled (a "continuance"), or that you were never notified of the hearing ("improper service"). You can file a Motion to Vacate Judgment anytime after the default, but judges generally aren't sympathetic unless you act immediately after you learn about the judgment.

PRETRIAL MANEUVERS

Sometimes the unexpected can happen on the morning of your trial. The other side might decide to settle out of court or at the last minute might ask to reschedule the hearing. If you're a plaintiff, you may find at the last minute that *you* are being sued by your opponent. It is important to know about such pretrial tactics and what to do about them.

Counterclaims

As we've seen, the person you're suing has a right to countersue. In some states, this counterclaim must be filed with the clerk before the trial, but elsewhere it can be made on the morning, or even at the beginning, of the trial.

If you live in a state where counterclaims must be filed in advance, it's worth calling the clerk before trial to see if one has been raised against you. If it has, ask the clerk to read you the reason for the counterclaim. This will allow you to bring to court additional evidence to oppose it.

If the person you're suing counterclaims just before the trial, you have two options. You can rely on your evidence and presentation to show the counterclaim is frivolous, or you can ask for a continuance. Judges almost always grant a continuance when additional evidence is needed to refute an unexpected counterclaim.

The most significant problem with counterclaims is that they sometimes seek more than the dollar limits of the court. In some states this automatically pushes the case into a higher, formal court. If this tactic is used on you, recognize that it's often used to intimidate plaintiffs: the other side may think you'll drop your case rather than take on the trouble and expense of hiring a lawyer and dealing with formal court procedures, delays and other hassles.

In some jurisdictions, a counterclaim over the dollar limit cannot push a case out of small claims court. Unfortunately, only a few courts follow this practice. If your court is not one of them, your only chance of preventing this maneuver— and it's a slim one—is to appeal to the judge. Judges see this maneuver being tried by lawyers in small claims courts all the time. Usually they recognize it as an attempt to prevent you from seeking simple and inexpensive justice. Your only hope is to appeal to the judge's sense of fairness. Respond to the counterclaim by telling your small claims court judge something like this:

> "Your Honor, I think the defendant and his [or her] attorney have made a counterclaim of this size simply because they want to move this case into formal court. They know that the cost of hiring a lawyer to continue this action in a higher court will make it uneconomical for me to pursue my claim. I request that you ask the defendant either to reduce the counterclaim to fit within the limits of this court, to demonstrate the grounds for a counterclaim of this size, or to file a separate suit in civil court."

If the judge is sympathetic, such an appeal might work. If not, you are no longer dealing with a small claims case. Your options at this point are to drop the case, hire a lawyer to handle it in civil court, or try to continue the case yourself in higher court.

The first option may seem to be grossly unfair, but if your claim is for $200 or less, the cost of continuing may be more than you'd recover. The second option is not unreasonable if you think you not only will win your case, but also collect attorneys' fees in the final judgment. The third option may work if you can find a lawyer to coach you on how to use the formal court. Remember, though, that if the other side has a lawyer and some basis for a counterclaim, you could lose not only your case but also end up paying expensive court costs.[1]

Pretrial Settlement

Don't be surprised if the other side offers to settle with you a few days—or even a few minutes—before your case goes to trial. You can almost count on this happening if the other side is represented by a lawyer.

Settlement offers are made when one side recognizes it may not or cannot win in court and decides instead to cut its losses. Whether or not you accept the offer should depend on its size and the strength of your case.

If the offer is made before the trial date, you may decide to accept payment of 75 percent of your claim rather than waste a business day in small claims court. Besides the nuisance of going to court, it's always possible you might not win. And even if you do win, you may not be given all you're claiming. According to Ruhnka and Weller, individuals who sued in consumer cases won, on average, only 68 percent of what they claimed. In landlord-tenant cases, plaintiffs won only slightly more, and in damage suits, they averaged 79 percent of what they sued for.

If the offer is made on the day of the trial, you can probably afford to be more demanding about what you'll settle for. After all, you've already taken the trouble to come to court and it won't be that much more difficult to settle the matter in front of the judge.

If you settle after the clerk's roll call but before you face the judge, the judge may still want to interview both you and your opponent, then enter the settlement in the court record. *Do not leave the courtroom* until you have an opportunity to tell the judge that a settlement has been reached, then ask the judge to note the settlement in your case record.

[1]See *Using a Lawyer* by Kay Ostberg in association with HALT, Random House, 1990, before consulting a lawyer about continuing your case.

Should you accept the settlement offer? That depends. If it is made by a lawyer for the other side, you can assume it's a double-barreled strategy. First, if the settlement is less than you sued for, the lawyer can "justify" the fee charged to the client by pointing to the money saved. Second, the lawyer will try to use your refusal as a sign that you did not behave reasonably in pretrial negotiations. If this happens, tell the judge you thought the settlement offer was too low when compared with your documented losses and that you decided to rely on the decision of the judge.

If you do decide to accept the settlement offer, whether from an attorney or directly from the opposing party, be sure to protect yourself. Say you will accept the settlement and drop your suit only if you receive cash or a check for the full agreed amount *before* the trial. Then get the settlement agreement in writing. It should look something like this:

It is agreed by (plaintiff) and (defendant), Plaintiff and Defendant in the case of (plaintiff) vs. (defendant), Docket No. _____, (year) in (name of court) of (location) that the above action will be settled for the sum of ($_____).

This sum was received in full by (plaintiff) from (defendant) on (date). In return for this sum, (plaintiff) will notify the court and discontinue the above action.

If the defendant defaults on this agreement, the plaintiff shall have the right to initiate court action to collect both the above sum and the additional costs of collection, including court costs and attorneys' fees.

Signed,

_____
Plaintiff

_____
Defendant

_____
Date

Having a written agreement will be crucial if the other side tries something like stopping payment on a check written on the day of the trial. If this happens, the original elements of your case (loss, liability, and so on) no longer matter. You now have a straightforward contract that the other side has broken. It will be easy to take this document to court and win a judgment. In fact, the costs of hiring a lawyer to do this for you are now covered by the contract.

Continuances

It's fairly easy to get a hearing date postponed, either by mutual consent or by a letter to the court. In most cases, postponements (called "continuances") are arranged well before the trial date, but they can be requested by either side at any point up until the judge renders a decision.

When a continuance is requested during the trial, it is usually because one side needs time to collect further evidence or testimony. When the continuance is requested on the morning of the trial (that is, when you unexpectedly find your name on the calendar's "motion" list), it's probably a stalling tactic. If the other side is represented by a lawyer, you can be fairly sure this is an attempt to complicate matters. If you suspect your opponent is stalling, tell the judge.

At the motion hearing, the other side will first be asked to explain why a continuance is needed, then you will be asked if you object to the continuance. Your best response will be something like this:

> "Your Honor, my telephone number and address are clearly given on both my initial letters of complaint to *(the other side)* and on the Plaintiff's Statement. The defendant has known about this trial date for two weeks. I could have been contacted by telephone or mail at any point before today and would have consented to a postponement. However, I've taken off from work and have gone to some trouble to arrange to be here this morning. Also, I have witnesses here who have taken the trouble to appear in court. I think the other side believes it can get me to drop this case if the number and nuisance of my court appearances can be increased. I ask that we hold the trial now and settle this matter today."

Most judges routinely consent to at least the first request for a continuance. However, the judge will listen to your objections and may well agree with you that the other side's reasons for requesting the continuance are weak.

Arbitration

Eleven states and the District of Columbia have small claims courts that offer arbitration or mediation programs. If you decided to try this option (page 18), you'll be given the opportunity to make this choice just before trial. But remember, the other side must also agree, unless you are suing in a state such as California, which makes arbitration mandatory on the defendant if the plaintiff chooses it. Also, remember that seeking court-sponsored arbitration might deny you any appeal rights.

If previous attempts at arbitration or pretrial settlement have failed, and if you have a solid case, you might as well tell it to the judge. After all, you're already in the courthouse.

CHAPTER 10

THE
TRIAL

If you've done a good job collecting the necessary evidence and planning your presentation, the trial will be short and simple. You probably have a good idea of how it works already. Unless your case is first on the docket, you will sit in the courtroom watching other small claims trials until the clerk calls your case. Then you, your opponent and all your witnesses will move to the front of the courtroom and take seats facing the judge.

Usually the clerk or judge begins by reading a summary of the case taken from your Plaintiff's Statement. You'll be sworn in, tell your story and present your evidence. The judge will probably ask you a few questions. Then your witnesses will be sworn in and will give their testimony.

After your witnesses speak, the person you are suing will be sworn in and makes a presentation. The defendants may be allowed to question you or your witnesses to bring out further facts. Then the defendant's witnesses are sworn and testify. You may be allowed to question the defendant or the defendant's witnesses. The judge may ask questions of both sides at any time during the hearing or may wait until everyone has spoken.

YOUR APPEARANCE

When it's your turn to face the judge, concentrate on your appearance. The trial will last only a few minutes and the evidence on some points may boil down to your word against your opponent's. For this reason, your behavior in court is crucial to your case. Judges call this "demeanor evidence," and they rely upon it to a great extent.

Remember that the judge knows absolutely nothing about you. A judge who has to determine if you behaved reasonably in the events that led to this trial will be guided largely by the impression you make in court. To make the best possible impression, try to follow these basic rules.

1. *Dress neatly.* Judges tend to be fairly conservative. They prefer to see people dressed "properly" for an appearance in court. Gaudy clothing, worn-out jeans, tee-shirts and the like will put you at a disadvantage with many judges.

2. *Stand.* Unless the judge has instructed otherwise, stand whenever you talk to the judge, tell your story or answer questions. Showing respect for the court means showing some respect for the judge.

3. *Be polite.* At all times, address the judge as "Your Honor," and answer "yes" or "no" questions with "Yes, Your Honor," and "No, Your Honor." If a lawyer is an acting judge for the day (a judge *pro tem*), then use "Sir" or "Ma'am." *Never* interrupt a judge, your opponent or a witness. You will have your chance to speak. *Never* argue with a judge. You can emphasize or repeat anything you think is important, but if the judge says the point is irrelevant, accept it and move on to your next point.

4. *Introduce yourself and your case.* If the judge was shuffling through papers when your name or case was called, or if the basis of your suit wasn't read aloud, introduce yourself

and *briefly* describe your case. Don't start reeling off facts until you're sure the judge has focused on the subject at hand.

5. *Be brief.* Stick to the essential facts and let your evidence speak for you.

6. *Be prepared.* If you need to show evidence in support of any assertion you make in your testimony, know how your materials are organized so the judge doesn't have to wait while you fumble through a stack of papers. If you are missing a crucial piece of evidence, be ready to explain its absence.

7. *Never read testimony.* Reading makes your testimony boring and unconvincing to the judge. Don't try to memorize anything. If you are afraid of forgetting important points, make notes or use an outline.

8. *Don't act like a lawyer.* This may be the most important rule of all. Many people sabotage their own cases by using legal terms they don't understand or by performing a ludicrous parody of Perry Mason. If you start acting like a lawyer, the judge may start treating you like one: the natural inclination to help you will disappear, and sympathy may pass to the other side. The first and last legal-sounding term you should utter in a courtroom is "Your Honor."

9. *Listen to the judge.* If the judge tells you to take a few extra minutes and try to settle the case out of court, take the hint. The judge probably means the facts or the law aren't on your side and your best bet is to get what you can through settlement.

10. *Remember your costs.* If you've incurred any special costs in bringing your case to court, be sure to tell the judge. You should specifically state at the end of your presentation that you would like a specified amount of money added to your award for these costs.

THE JUDGMENT

After listening to both sides, the judge may discuss the merits of each side's case. Then, depending on the judge and the jurisdiction, the judge will either announce the verdict in court or indicate that both sides will be notified by mail.

Courtroom Verdicts If the judge announces the decision in court—and this is unusual—it will be easier to arrange payment or collection of the award. If you are the one who owes the money, you can either pay the amount in full, arrange a payment plan with the plaintiff or ask the judge to order installment payments. If you pay while still at the courthouse, be sure to get your opponent to sign a "Satisfaction of Judgment" form.

A Satisfaction of Judgment form is usually available from the court clerk's office. If not, you can quickly draft one yourself. It must include the name and district of the court, the names of the plaintiff and defendant and the case number. It should say something like this:

I acknowledge full satisfaction of the judgment in (plaintiff) vs. (defendant), case no. ———, in (name of court) of (location). Satisfaction was executed at (city/county), (state), on (date). The sum of ——————————— dollars and cents ($———·———) was received from (defendant) at this time.

Signature

JUDGMENT CREDITOR

The Satisfaction of Judgment should be signed by the person who receives the money (the judgment creditor) upon receipt. If you are the one paying, it is important that you get a copy of the Satisfaction of Judgment for yourself, plus one for the court. Filing a copy with the court clerk will prevent your opponent from taking you to court over the same matter again. Keeping a copy could also be important if you later need to clear your credit record.

If you have convinced the judge to allow payment by installments, be sure to get a signed Satisfaction of Judgment statement once you make the last payment and file a copy with the court. When you pay on an installment plan, always pay in a way that gives you a record—canceled checks or money orders, for example.

If you win your case, try to collect payment while you're still in the courthouse. It's much easier to do in person just after a verdict than later by telephone or mail. Speak with the defendant in the hallway outside the courtroom. Offer to complete and sign the Satisfaction of Judgment form on the spot and clear the judgment immediately, or make a definite arrangement for payment with the defendant before you leave court. Set a deadline for payment, and promise a Satisfaction of Judgment form in return. It may be easier to arrange if you agree to accept installments.

Verdicts by Mail

In most states, the judge's decision is not announced in court but is sent by mail to both sides. If you receive notice in the mail that you've won, contact the other side immediately and arrange payment. A postcard from the courthouse is not forceful when it comes to encouraging someone to pay, so it's important to act while the authority of the judge is fresh in the defendant's mind. Offer a Satisfaction of Judgment form upon payment in full or at the conclusion of the installment payments, and mention alternative collection procedures if you detect hesitation.

If you were the defendant and are notified that you've lost, you can either pay the amount in full or seek an installment plan. If you can afford only to pay on installments, contact the person who sued you and see if you can arrange a private agreement. Find out how much you'll have to pay per week or month and get an agreement in writing.

If your opponent will not agree to an installment plan and you must have one, ask the judge to order one. Call the court clerk and ask if you must arrange a hearing or if a letter to the judge will suffice. If you must write a letter, be sure to include the name and the docket number of the case, the size of the judgment, and the reason why you can't pay the amount in a lump sum. Say how much you can afford to pay per month and ask that the original order be changed to incorporate this payment schedule. For more information on getting a court-ordered payment plan, speak to the court clerk.

CHAPTER 11

APPEALS

If you feel the judge's verdict was unfair or based on an error, in some states you can appeal your case. The small claims courts of Arizona, Connecticut, Hawaii, Louisiana's City Court, North Dakota, Oregon's District Court, and South Dakota do not permit appeals. California, Massachusetts, New York, Oregon's Justice Court and Rhode Island allow only the defendant to appeal a case. The remaining states, Virgin Islands, Puerto Rico and the District of Columbia permit an appeal by either side, but each state has its own special appeal provisions (see Appendix 1).

TYPES OF APPEALS

In more than half the states (including some courts in Georgia, Louisiana, Montana, Oregon and Wyoming), the appeal is *de novo*. This means simply that the first trial is scrapped and the case begins again, from the beginning, in a formal civil court. You will have to present your evidence and witnesses much like you did in small claims court, although the first trial should have taught you how to strengthen your case or presentation. Remember that civil court rules are much more complex than those in small claims court. They involve discovery, formal pleadings and the like. The cost and delay can be considerable.

In the remaining states that allow appeals, the appeal must be based on questions of law, not on the facts of the case. In these states, it's not enough to appeal because you disagree with the judge about the quality of your evidence or the appearance of false testimony. You can only appeal if you can demonstrate that the judge misapplied the law. An example of this would be a consumer case in which a judge failed to recognize the immunity from liability provided by a federal consumer protection statute.

The reasoning behind an appeal of law is usually difficult for nonlawyers to recognize. Further practical problems arise because you'll need a court record. The appeal judge must be able to see the basis for the small claims judge's decision, but, unfortunately, small claims proceedings seldom include making a stenographic or audio recording. Most judges make bench notes during a small claims trial, however, and these are often accepted as a sufficient record. If they are not, the appellate court will either refuse to grant an appeal or order a new trial.

FILING AN APPEAL

Time is crucial when you are seeking an appeal. In most states, you have only two or three weeks in which to file an appeal of a small claims court decision. If you received notice of the small claims judgment by mail, you may only have a few days before the deadline is past.

To file the appeal, complete a "Notice to Appeal" statement in the court clerk's office. Give the name of your case, the reason for your appeal and the amount of the small claims judgment against you or, if you were the plaintiff, the amount of money you were claiming. You'll have to pay a filing fee of $25 to $100. (Everything is more expensive in formal civil court.) Some courts will require you to post a bond in the amount of the small claims judgment you're appealing to assure that you will pay if you lose a second time. The bond may also be required to cover such court costs as for a jury or court reporters.

After you've filed and paid the fee, the court will notify the other side and a trial will be scheduled for about a month later. Some districts (as in Iowa, Wyoming and the District of Columbia) have a review court that can reject a ground-less appeal without a hearing. In the District of Columbia, fifty-three out of sixty-two appeals from small claims court were refused in 1988. For more information about the appeal procedures in your state, see Appendix I.

SHOULD YOU APPEAL?

Appeals from small claims to formal civil courts are costly, complicated and risky. If you lose a second time, you will have to pay the original judgment and perhaps the court costs for the second trial.

It is important that you seek some form of legal help before you commit yourself to an appeal. This is especially important if your appeal is on a question of law. You must be sure that you have grounds for an appeal. You will proba-bly have to state those grounds in a legal brief for the ap-peals judge.

You should seek some sort of legal help even if your appeal is for a new trial. After all, you lost the first time around. If you're going to win in a second trial, you'll need someone's help in organizing and preparing your presenta-tion. Also, appellate judges tend to look upon people who appeal small claims cases as "sore losers." You'll need a significantly better case the second time around if you're to overcome this sort of prejudice.

Appeals from small claims court make sense *only* if a great amount of money is at stake and *only* if you have confirmed that you have a solid basis for an appeal. Otherwise, take the opportunity to cut your losses.

CHAPTER 12

COLLECTING
THE AWARD

Unfortunately, winning a judgment in small claims court isn't the end of the matter. You now have to collect what you've won. Sometimes that's not too difficult—you may even get a check from the losing party before leaving the courthouse. Sadly, though, many winners must not only wait to collect what's due but must actively track it down. They soon realize that taking a case through small claims court is not difficult—it's collecting the award that is.

If the appeal period has expired and it's clear that the person the court ordered to pay you the award will not pay willingly, you may have to take additional steps to collect it. Your defendant has turned into a debtor—in legal jargon, your "judgment debtor." Unfortunately, most small claims courts have no established procedures for enforcing their judgments. The small claims clerk will be able to tell you about collection rules for your state, but the task of collecting is yours, not the court's.

Collecting small claims judgments can be troublesome. The procedure is time-consuming and can be complicated and expensive. According to Ruhnka and Weller, two thirds to three fourths of all plaintiffs collect when both sides go to court to contest the case. When the person being sued doesn't show up for court and the plaintiff wins by default, the results are very different. Only one fourth to one half of plaintiffs collect their awards.

If more people knew about the collection options available to them, the success rate could be considerably higher. Because collection procedures are defined both by state law and by the specific practices of the local court and sheriff's office, the following guide must be general. For more specific information, ask your small claims clerk, the clerk of the higher civil court or someone from the sheriff's or marshal's office.

WRIT OF EXECUTION

To collect any money or property to cover what is owed you, you'll need a court order called a "Writ of Execution." Take your judgment to the small claims clerk to fill out an application for a Writ of Execution. You'll have to pay a small fee, which is recoverable, then wait perhaps a few days for a judge to sign your writ. The writ is the judge's order to a sheriff or marshal to collect any of the debtor's assets needed to satisfy the judgment. It will have an expiration date, usually thirty to ninety days from the date it was signed.

Before it expires, take the writ to the sheriff's or marshal's office in the county where the offices are located. Keep the original and give copies of the writ to the sheriff or marshal, along with payment of a fee for collection. The amount of the fee will depend on the type of asset you're asking the sheriff to collect.

The sheriff or marshal will either give you a form or ask that you write a letter stating your name, the small claims case's name and number, the amount of the judgment, the debtor's name and address and the location and description of the assets you want seized. You may consider claiming the following types of assets:

Automobiles You can ask that a debtor's car be seized and sold at a sheriff's auction. First, contact the Department of Motor Vehicles for your county or state to determine whether your debtor is the registered owner of the car. Also check to see if he or she still owes money on the car. If the debtor has only paid $1,000 on the car, then the debtor's "equity" in the car is $1,000, and you can collect no more than that after an auction. In fact, you'll get less than that, because every state excludes a part of car owner's equity from seizure. Thus, in a state that protects $750 in equity, you'd collect only $250 of the $1,000. Expect the amount of protected equity to be even higher if the car is a "tool of trade" used by the debtor to earn a living. Also, remember that an auction is not likely to bring the full value of the car. After the auction fees and other costs are deducted, there may be little or nothing left for you.

Bank Accounts   If you know where the debtor banks, ask the sheriff to go to the bank and empty a debtor's checking or savings account. In some states, you'll have to know the account number. Special provisions may apply if it is a joint account or a business account or if it has any special exemptions. If you do not know where the debtor banks, see "Locating the Debtor's Assets" below.

Business Assets   You may have ways of collecting from judgment debtors that are businesses. Besides seizing bank accounts, you can have a sheriff go to the business and empty the cash register, or seize all the money collected during one business day. You cannot have the sheriff seize business property. Such property helps the debtor make a living and is therefore protected against collectors. Basically, that means you can take the cash, but not the cash register.

The cost of hiring someone to collect for you are fairly high, but if you succeed you can be reimbursed for them. Some states have special punitive damages you may collect from a business that ignores a court judgment. Check with the small claims clerk about this.

Personal Property   You are permitted to seize some of the person's personal possessions, but in practice this is difficult to do. For one thing, state laws exempt many things from seizure—everything from furniture and clothing to television sets. Further, the property may belong to someone else, for example, a roommate or other creditors who may have a prior claim. For these reasons, sheriffs and marshals dislike seizing personal property and may make you post an attachment bond of $1,000 or more should conflicting claims of ownership arise.

Real Property   Real estate may be difficult to seize and sell, but land-owning debtors can easily be pressured into paying. Simply pay the small claims clerk to give you an "Abstract of Judgment" and file this wherever title to the debtor's land is kept—usually the County Records Office. This places a *lien* on the title to the property. The debtor will be unable to sell the land until he or she clears the title by paying you. Of course, you needn't wait until the debtor tries to sell the land. Simply notify the debtor and the bank that holds the mortgage that you have a lien on the property. This usually brings quick results.

Wages   Finally, you can have the sheriff or marshal contact the debtor's employer to order that the debtor's wages be garnished. This means that, until the debt is paid off, the employer will have to deduct a percentage from the debtor's paycheck each week and send it to you. Garnishment is not allowed in a few states, and it is usually prohibited when the wages are needed to support a low-income family. For more information on each state's laws governing garnishment of a person's wages, check *Collier on Bankruptcy* [1] at a local law library. It's a ten-volume set with an entire volume dedicated to state exemptions from garnishment.

---

[1] *Collier on Bankruptcy,* 15th edition, Mathew Bender, New York, 1979.

LOCATING THE DEBTOR'S ASSETS

So far we have assumed that the judgment debtor has certain assets and that you know where they are located. This is not always the case. If you need more information about the existence or location of assets, you can ask the court to examine the debtor's assets. To do this, ask the clerk for an "Order of Examination of Assets." (As usual, the actual name varies from state to state.) Complete this form and pay a fee. After a judge signs the form, have it delivered to the debtor by personal service. For another fee, a sheriff, marshal or other professional process server should be able to do this for you. All these costs should be recoverable in the end.

If the debtor is properly served, failure to appear in court usually results in being cited for contempt of court. That means a bench warrant will be issued for the debtor's arrest. Given the serious consequences if they don't, most debtors show up this time around. It's probably worth ordering a reluctant debtor to come to court and disclose assets just for the shock value. The debtor may even pay before having to tell all to the judge. If not, the examination will give you a better idea of where the debtor's assets are located.

Often the judge questions the debtor directly, but sometimes dozens of such examinations are in progress in the courtroom at the same time, usually conducted by creditors' lawyers. In this situation, you'll have to question the debtor yourself and report to the judge. Be sure to ask the debtor about all the assets we have discussed and find out where they are located. If the debtor is being evasive, tell the judge. The debtor will be put on the stand for questioning by the judge. Also, ask if the debtor is carrying any cash. You can ask that this be handed over to you in court.

JUDGMENT-PROOF DEBTORS

Sometime a judgment debtor has no job, no income and no assets that can be seized. This sort of debtor is said to be "judgment proof." You have no way to collect a judgment immediately. The other type of judgment-proof debtor is a defendant who moves after a judgment and leaves no forwarding address.

You are most likely to encounter a judgment-proof debtor in default cases. They don't appear in court because they've already moved or know you won't be able to collect from them. However, a small claims judgment is good for five to ten years, and you can have the debtor hauled into court every six months for an examination of assets. The debtor will probably acquire at least some assets over time, and the mere threat of being periodically dragged into court should be an incentive to pay.

COSTS AFTER JUDGMENT

Any costs you incurred before the small claims judgment was issued should have been added to your claim when you asked for costs in court. Most costs incurred in trying to collect the judgment can also be collected from the debtor— as long as it is possible to collect anything. In many states, you can ask that these costs be added to the amount ordered collected in the Writ of Execution. Bear in mind that some fees can be collected only *after* you file a collection motion with the judge. You must then collect these fees as if they were a separate judgment. This is unlikely to be worth the effort unless you've spent a considerable sum.

An expensive way of collecting a judgment is to have a collection agency or collection attorney try to collect it for you. Both commonly take a third to half of whatever they manage to collect from the debtor, plus expenses. If you don't have time to track down an elusive debtor or the debtor's assets, you might want to consider this option, but it makes sense only if a lot of money is at stake, if collection has proven too difficult and time-consuming and if you're willing to accept two thirds to half (minus collection costs) of the total judgment.

If you plan to go this route, contact a collection agency. These companies use nonlawyer collectors and have established records of obeying the federal fair practice rules that govern the way debts can be collected. Until recently, collection attorneys were exempt from these rules and were thus able to use unfair, and sometimes unethical collection practices on debtors. Lawyers are no longer exempt from the Fair Debt Collection Practices Act (FDCPA). They are now required to obey the same rules as nonlawyer debt collectors.

The American Collectors Association, Inc., 4040 West 70th Street, Minneapolis, MN 55435, (612) 926-6547, and the Associated Credit Bureaus, Inc., 16211 Park 10 Place, Houston, TX 77084, (713) 492-8155, are trade associations that can tell you how to contact nonlawyer collectors. You can also contact nonlawyer collectors by looking under "collection agencies" in your yellow pages.

If you decide to hire a collection lawyer, ask the court clerk for the names of several in your area and shop for the one who offers a reasonable percentage arrangement and also has a reputation for honesty. Be sure to ask if you'll have to pay a fee if the lawyer doesn't collect anything.

Conclusion

Going to court—any court—may not be the best way to resolve your legal difficulties. As we have seen in this book, even when your problem seems to fit the criteria for the small claims court in your state, other methods of resolving your problem may be preferable. Small claims court, however, does offer a reasonably simple, inexpensive and, in most instances, fair way to get a just settlement.

The purpose of this book has been to enable you to make your way through small claims court as an informed and confident consumer, without the need for the services of expensive professionals. If you are involved in a dispute that can be resolved by an award of money, you should now be prepared to take the matter to small claims court.

The truth is that the more people use small claims courts, the more responsive these courts will be to the needs of the public. Already many states have moved to simplify procedures: by distributing brochures and videotapes that explain local rules and processes; by extending court hours to evenings and weekends; by increasing the dollar limit for cases to be brought; by barring attorneys from the courtroom; and by providing alternative dispute resolution programs.

There may, in fact, be an even more significant ripple effect from the use of small claims courts. Perhaps the steps being taken to streamline and increase access to these "people's courts" will someday also be applied to the higher courts. In that event, justice would be better served.

APPENDIXES

STATE RULES

This appendix gives some of the special rules that apply to the small claims courts of all fifty states, the District of Columbia, Puerto Rico and the Virgin Islands. All the terms and concepts below are explained in either the text or the glossary. Filing fees are not listed because they vary greatly and change frequently.

All data, except "dollar limits," were compiled in October 1989. The data on dollar limits were compiled in December 1989. Because court rules may change at any time, always check with the clerk of the small claims court to verify the accuracy of the information given for your state.

Additional information on small claims court rules is found under each state's "Special Provisions" section. If that section for your state does not cover a particular rule (for example, the right to a jury trial), you should check with your small claims clerk. Where there is no small claims court or section in a state, check with the clerk of the court named.

Alabama   Small Claims (District Court)
Statutes: Code of Alabama 1986 (amendments to 1989), Title 12, Ch. 12, Sections 31, 70–71; Alabama Rules of Courts; Small Claims Rules.
Dollar Limit: $1,000.
Where to Sue: Where defendant resides or injury occurred. Corporation resides where it does business.
Service: Certified mail, sheriff or court-approved adult.
Hearing Date: Set by court.

Attorneys: Allowed; required for assignees.

Transfer: No provision.

Appeals: By either side for new trial; to Circuit Court within 14 days.

Special Provisions: Limited equitable relief available. Defendant must answer within 14 days or lose by default.

Alaska   Small Claims (District Court)

Statutes: Alaska Statutes 1988 (amendments to 1989), Title 22, Ch. 15, Section 040; District Court Rules of Civil Procedure, Rules 18–22. Alaska Rules of Civil Procedure, Rule 4.

Dollar Limit: $5,000.

Where to Sue: Court nearest defendant's residence or place of employment, or where injury occurred.

Service: Certified or registered mail (binding on defendant who refuses to accept) or peace officer.

Hearing Date: Not less than 15 days from service.

Attorneys: Allowed; required for assignees.

Transfer: Check with clerk of court.

Appeals: By either side for review of law, not facts; to Superior Court within 30 days.

Special Provisions: Equitable relief available. Defendant must file written answer within 20 days of service or lose by default. Arbitration may be ordered in counterclaims for less than $3,000. Court may order installment payments.

Arizona   Small Claims Division (Justice Court)

Statutes: Arizona Revised Statutes 1975 (amendments to 1988), Sections 22.501–523, 22.202 a–e.

Dollar Limit: $1,000.

Where to Sue: Where defendant resides. Intentional torts: where act occurred. To recover personal property: where property is. Contracts: where performance expected. Nonresident defendants: where plaintiff resides. Transient defendants: where found.

Service: Certified or registered mail, sheriff, deputy or court-approved adult.

Hearing Date: Set by court; within 60 days of the filing of the answer.

Attorneys: Not allowed unless both sides agree in writing.

Transfer: If either side requests or if defendant counterclaims for more than $500, case tried under regular civil procedure of court.

Appeals: Not allowed.

Special Provisions: Limited equitable relief available. Defendant must answer within 20 days or lose by default. No discovery. No jury trial. No libel or slander, forcible entry or unlawful detainer, specific performance, prejudgment remedies, injunctions, cases against the state or cases involving ownership of real estate. Right to sue may not be transferred.

Arkansas Small Claims Division (Municipal Court)

Statutes: Arkansas Code of 1987 (annotated) (amendments to 1989), Title 16.17, Sections 201–210, 218, 601–614; Inferior Court Rules; Constitutions; Arkansas Constitution Amendment 64.

Dollar Limit: $3,000.

Where to Sue: Where defendant resides or injury occurred. Contracts: where performance expected. Corporation resides where it does business.

Service: Certified mail, sheriff or court-approved adult.

Hearing Date: 30–45 days after summons issued.

Attorneys: Not allowed.

Transfer: If attorney appears or if defendant files compulsory counterclaim for more than $3,000, case tried under regular civil procedure of Municipal Court.

Appeals: By either side for new trial; to Circuit Court within 30 days.

Special Provisions: Collection agents and commercial lenders may not sue. Corporations limited to 12 claims a year. Right to sue may not be transferred.

California Small Claims Division (Justice or Municipal Court)

Statutes: Annotated California Codes, Code of Civil Procedure 1982 (amendments to 1989), Sections 116–117.22.

Dollar Limit: $2,000; $2,500 after Jan. 1, 1991.

Where to Sue: Where defendant resides or injury occurred. Contracts: where performance expected. Consumer contracts: where signed. Corporation resides where it does business.

Service: Certified or registered mail, sheriff or court-approved adult.

Hearing Date: Defendant in county: 10–40 days after summons issued. Defendant outside county: 30–70 days after summons issued.

Attorneys: Not allowed unless attorney represents self.

Transfer: If defendant counterclaims for more than $2,000, counterclaim removed to higher court if judge permits.

Appeals: By defendant only for new trial; to Superior Court within 20 days.

Special Provisions: Equitable relief available. Right to sue may not be transferred. Judge may determine payment schedule. Interpreters available. Small claims advisor available at no cost. Court may order arbitration.

Colorado   Small Claims Division (County Court)
Statutes: Colorado Revised Statutes 1973 (amendments to 1987), Sections 13.6.401–413; Colorado Rules of Civil Procedure for Small Claims Courts, Rules 501–521.
Dollar Limit: $2,000.
Where to Sue: Where defendant resides or injury occurred. Contracts: for sale of goods, where sold; for debt or installment purchases of personal or household goods, where contract signed; for services, where services were to be performed. Nonresident defendants: where defendant found or plaintiff resides.
Service: Certified mail, sheriff, deputy or court-approved disinterested adult.
Hearing Date: Set by court; at least 21 days after summons issued.
Attorneys: Not allowed unless attorney represents self or as full-time employee of partnership or corporation involved in the case. If attorney appears, other side may also have attorney.
Transfer: If defendant counterclaims for more than $2,000 or wants to use an attorney, case tried under regular civil procedure of court.
Appeals: By either side for review of law, not facts; to District Court within 15 days.
Special Provisions: No equitable relief except nullification of contracts. No jury trial. No libel or slander, forcible entry or detainer, recovery of personal property, specific performance, prejudgment attachment, injunctions or traffic cases. Right to sue may not be transferred. No discovery. Limit of 2 claims a month per plaintiff or 18 claims a year. Referee may be appointed.

Connecticut   Small Claims (Superior Court)
Statutes: Connecticut General Statutes Annotated 1985 (amendments to 1989), Title 51, Section 15; Title 52, Sections 549a–d.
Dollar Limit: $2,000.
Where to Sue: Where defendant resides, does business or where injury occurred. Contracts: where breach occurred or obligation incurred. Landlord-tenant: where premises are located.
Service: Registered or certified mail or sheriff.
Hearing Date: Set by court.
Attorneys: Allowed.
Transfer: If defendant requests and court approves, to regular civil procedure of Superior Court.

Appeals: Not allowed.

Special Provisions: No equitable relief. No libel or slander. Litigants may submit matter to county commissioner for binding decision.

Delaware   No small claims procedure (Justice of the Peace)

Statutes: Delaware Code Annotated 1974 (amendments to 1988), Title 10, Sections 9301–9590.

Dollar Limit: $2,500.

Where to Sue: Any county.

Service: Certified mail, sheriff, deputy or constable.

Hearing Date: Set by court.

Attorneys: Allowed.

Transfer: No provision.

Appeals: By either side for new trial in cases involving more than $5; to Superior Court within 15 days.

Special Provisions: Jury trial available.

District of Columbia   Small Claims and Conciliation Branch (Superior Court)

Statutes: District of Columbia Code 1981 (amendments to 1989), Title 11, Sections 1301–1323; Title 16, Sections 3901–3910; Rules for Small Claims and Conciliation.

Dollar Limit: $2,000.

Where to Sue: Only one court in District.

Service: Certified or registered mail, U.S. marshal or court-approved disinterested adult.

Hearing Date: 5–15 days from filing of complaint.

Attorneys: Allowed; required for corporations.

Transfer: If either side requests jury trial, if defendant files counterclaim affecting ownership of real estate, or if court determines interest of justice requires it, case tried under regular civil procedure of court.

Appeals: By either side for review of law, not facts; to Court of Appeals within 3 days.

Special Provisions: No equitable relief. Limited discovery available with court permission. Court may refer cases to arbitration or mediation. Court may order installment payments. Wednesday evening and Saturday morning office hours available.

Florida   Summary Procedure (County Court)

Statutes: Florida Rules of Court (1989): Small Claims Rules, Rules 7.010–7.341; Florida Statute Annotated (amendments to 1989), Section 51.011.

Dollar Limit: $2,500.

Where to Sue: Where defendant resides or injury occurred. Contracts: where agreed, if contract provides; where unsecured note was signed or where maker resides; where breach occurred. To recover property: where property is. U.S. corporation resides where it maintains office for customary business. Foreign corporation resides where it has an agent.

Service: Registered mail (Florida residents only), peace officer or court-approved disinterested adult.

Hearing Date: Within 60 days after pretrial conference set by the court.

Attorneys: Allowed; required for collection agents and assignees.

Transfer: If defendant counterclaims for more than $2,500, case tried under regular civil procedure of County Court.

Appeals: By either side for review of law, not facts; to circuit court within 30 days.

Special Provisions: Equitable relief available. Jury trial available. Party represented by attorney is subject to discovery.

Georgia   No small claims procedure (Magistrate Court)

Statutes: Georgia Code Annotated 1985 (amendments to 1989), Title 15, Sections 10.1, 10.20, 10.40–137.

Dollar Limit: $5,000.

Where to Sue: Where defendant resides.

Service: Constable or court-approved adult.

Hearing Date: Set by court.

Attorneys: Allowed.

Transfer: If defendant counterclaims for more than $5,000, case tried in appropriate court depending on amount.

Appeals: By either side for new trial; to Superior Court within 30 days.

Special Provisions: Equitable relief available. Defendant must answer within 30 days or lose by default. No jury trial. Court may order installment payments.

Hawaii   Small Claims Division (District Court)

Statutes: Hawaii Revised Statutes 1985 (amendments to 1988), Title 34, Sections 633.27–36.

Dollar Limit: $2,500. Recovery of leased personal property valued less than $1,500 if rent due is less than $2,500. Security deposit disputes: no limit.

Where to Sue: Where defendant resides or where breach or injury occurred.

Service: Certified or registered mail if defendant resides within circuit. Otherwise, by sheriff, deputy, chief of police or court-appointed process server.

Hearing Date: Set by court.

Attorneys: Allowed, except in landlord-tenant cases. Nonattorney may represent party if no fee is charged.

Transfer: If either side requests jury trial or if defendant counterclaims for more than $5,000 and requests a jury trial, case tried in Circuit Court.

Appeals: Not allowed.

Special Provisions: No equitable relief except in landlord-tenant cases, in which jurisdiction is limited to orders to repair, replace, refund, reform and rescind.

Idaho   Small Claims Department (Magistrate's Division of the District Court)

Statutes: Idaho Code 1985 (amendments to 1989), Title 1, Sections 2301–2315.

Dollar Limit: $2,000.

Where to Sue: Where defendant resides or where breach or injury occurred.

Service: Certified or registered mail, sheriff or court-approved adult.

Hearing Date: Set by court; at least 14 days from service.

Attorneys: Not allowed.

Transfer: No provision.

Appeals: By either side for new trial; within 30 days to an "attorney magistrate."

Special Provisions: No jury trial. Right to sue may not be transferred.

Illinois   Small Claims (Circuit Court)

Statutes: Illinois Annotated Statutes 1985 (amendments to 1989), Ch. 110A, Sections 281–289.

Dollar Limit: $2,500.

Where to Sue: Where defendant resides or injury occurred. Contracts: where performance expected.

Service: Registered mail (if defendant resides within county of suit), sheriff or court-approved adult.

Hearing Date: Within 40 days after summons issued.

Attorneys: Allowed; required for corporations.

Transfer: No provision.

Appeals: By either side for review of law, not facts; to Appellate Court within 30 days.

Special Provisions: Cook County has a special *pro se* branch for cases involving less than $1,000. Attorneys not allowed in *pro se* branch. Jury trial available at request of defendant in Cook County and to either side elsewhere. Court may order installment payments. Court may order arbitration.

Indiana   Small Claims Division (Circuit Court)

Statutes: West's Annotated Indiana Code 1983 (amendments to 1988), Title 33, Sections 5-1 to 5-7, 11.6-1-1 to 11.6-1-7, 11.6-4-1 to 11.6-9-5; Indiana Practice; Rules of Procedure (Annotated).

Dollar Limit: $3,000.

Where to Sue: Where defendant resides or injury occurred. Contracts: where obligation incurred or performance expected.

Service: Registered mail; if that fails, sheriff or peace officer.

Hearing Date: Set by court.

Attorneys: Allowed.

Transfer: If defendant requests jury trial, case tried under regular civil procedure of appropriate court.

Appeals: By either side for review of law, not facts; to Court of Appeals within 20 days.

Special Provisions: No equitable relief. No jury trial. Defendant must file written answer within time set by court or lose by default. Court may order installment payments. Evening sessions available.

Iowa   Small Claims (District Court)

Statutes: Iowa Code Annotated 1964 (amendments to 1989), Sections 631.1–17 and Appendix.

Dollar Limit: $2,000.

Where to Sue: Where defendant resides or injury occurred. Contracts: where obligation incurred. Negotiable instruments: where issuer resides. Nonresident defendants: where found. Corporation resides where it has an office or agent.

Service: Certified or registered mail, peace officer or court-approved disinterested adult.

Hearing Date: Defendant must appear within 20 days; hearing set within 5–20 days thereafter.

Attorneys: Allowed.

Transfer: If defendant requests jury trial or counterclaims for more than $2,000 and judge permits, case tried under regular civil procedure of court.

Appeals: By either side for review of law, not facts; to District Court within 20 days.

Special Provisions: No equitable relief. No jury trial. Resident defendants have 20 days and nonresidents have 60 days to answer or lose by default. Written pleadings not required. Court may order installment payments.

Kansas Small Claims (District Court)
Statutes: Kansas Statutes Annotated 1983 (amendments to 1988), Sections 61.2701–2713.
Dollar Limit: $1,000.
Where to Sue: Where defendant resides or has a place of business or employment. Corporation resides where it transacts business or maintains registered office or resident agent.
Service: Sheriff, deputy, attorney or court-approved adult.
Hearing Date: Set by court.
Attorneys: Not allowed.
Transfer: If defendant counterclaims for more than $1,000 but less than dollar limit of District Court, judge will decide case or allow defendant to transfer to court of competent jurisdiction.
Appeals: By either side for new trial; to District Court within 10 days.
Special Provisions: Limit of 10 claims a year per plaintiff. Right to sue may not be transferred. No discovery. Collection agents may not sue.

Kentucky Small Claims Division (District Court)
Statutes: Kentucky Revised Statutes 1986 (amendments to 1988), Ch. 24A.200–360.
Dollar Limit: $1,500.
Where to Sue: Where defendant resides or does business.
Service: Certified or registered mail. If that fails, sheriff or constable.
Hearing Date: 20–40 days from service.
Attorneys: Allowed.
Transfer: If defendant counterclaims for more than $1,500 or requests jury trial or at judge's discretion, case tried under regular civil procedure of District Court or Circuit Court.
Appeals: By either side for review of law, not facts; to Circuit Court within 10 days.
Special Provisions: Limited equitable relief available. Limit of 25 claims a year per plaintiff. Collection agents and lenders of money at interest may not sue. No discovery.

Louisiana   Urban: Small Claims Division (City Court); rural: no small claims procedure (Justice of the Peace)

Statutes: Louisiana Statutes Annotated 1968 (amendments to 1989), Sections 13.5200–5211; Code of Civil Procedure 1961 (amendments to 1989), Articles 4831, 4911–4925.

Dollar Limit: $2,000.

Where to Sue: Where defendant resides. Corporation resides where it has an office or business establishment.

Service: City Court: certified mail, sheriff or constable. Justice of the peace: sheriff or constable.

Hearing Date: Set by court.

Attorneys: Allowed.

Transfer: City Court: if defendant counterclaims for more than $2,000, case tried under regular civil procedure of court. Justice of the Peace: no provision.

Appeals: City Court: not allowed. Justice of the Peace: by either side for new trial; to District Court within 15 days.

Special Provisions: City Court: equitable relief available. No jury trial. Case may be referred to arbitration if both sides consent. Court may order installment payments. Justice of the Peace: no equitable relief. Defendant must answer within 10 days or may lose by default. No cases involving ownership of real estate or family law.

Maine   Small Claims (District Court)

Statutes: Maine Revised Statutes Annotated 1964 (amendments to 1989), Title 14, Sections 1901, 7481–7485; Maine Rules of Small Claims Procedure, Rules 1–18.

Dollar Limit: $1,400.

Where to Sue: Where defendant resides or has a place of business or where transaction occurred. Corporate defendants: where agent resides.

Service: Certified or registered mail, sheriff or court-approved adult.

Hearing Date: Set by court.

Attorneys: Allowed.

Transfer: No removal of small claims to Superior Court allowed.

Appeals: By either side; to Superior Court within 10 days. Plaintiff's appeal will review law, not facts. Defendant's will be a new trial.

Special Provisions: No equitable relief except orders to return, reform, refund, repair, or rescind. No jury trial. Court may order mediation. No cases involving ownership of real estate.

Maryland   Small Claims (District Court)

Statutes: Annotated Code of Maryland 1986 (amendments to 1988), Courts and Judicial Proceedings Article, Section 4-405; Maryland Rules of Civil Procedure, Rule 3-701.

Dollar Limit: $2,500.

Where to Sue: Where defendant resides, has regular business or is employed, or where injury occurred. To recover personal property: where property is. Nonresident individual defendants: any county. Nonresident corporate defendants: where plaintiff resides. Corporation resides where principal office is.

Service: Certified mail, sheriff or any adult (may be an attorney for a party).

Hearing Date: Set by court; at least 60 days from filing of complaint, 90 days for out-of-state defendants.

Attorneys: Allowed.

Transfer: If either side requests jury trial, case tried in Circuit Court. If defendant counterclaims for more than $2,500, case tried under regular civil procedure of court.

Appeals: By either side for new trial; to Circuit Court within 30 days.

Special Provisions: No discovery.

Massachusetts   Small Claims (Boston: Municipal Court; elsewhere: District Court)

Statutes: Annotated Laws of Massachusetts 1986 (amendments to 1989), Ch. 218, Sections 21–25.

Dollar Limit: $1,500 (no limit for property damage caused by motor vehicles).

Where to Sue: Where plaintiff or defendant resides or where defendant has regular business or is employed. Landlord-tenant cases: where property is.

Service: Certified or registered mail.

Hearing Date: Set by court.

Attorneys: Allowed.

Transfer: If defendant requests jury trial or in judge's discretion, case tried under regular civil procedure of appropriate court.

Appeals: By defendant only for new trial; to Superior Court within 10 days.

Special Provisions: No equitable relief. No libel or slander cases. Court may refer cases to mediation if both sides agree.

Michigan   Small Claims Division (District Court)

Statutes: Michigan Statutes Annotated 1986 (amendments to 1989–90), Ch. 27A, Sections 8401–8427.

Dollar Limit: $1,500.

Where to Sue: Where defendant resides or where breach or injury occurred.

Service: Certified mail or disinterested adult.

Hearing Date: 15–45 days from service.

Attorneys: Not allowed.

Transfer: If either side requests or defendant counterclaims for more than $1,500, case tried under regular civil procedure of court.

Appeals: If trial was before District Court magistrate, by either side for new trial; to small claims District Court judge within 7 days. Otherwise, not allowed.

Special Provisions: No equitable relief. Right to sue may not be transferred. No libel or slander, intentional torts or fraud cases. No jury trial. Limit of 5 claims a year per plaintiff. Court may refer cases to mediation or arbitration.

Minnesota   Conciliation Court (County Court)

Statutes: Minnesota Statutes Annotated 1971 (amendments to 1989), Section 487.30; Rules for the Conciliation Court, Rules 1.01–1.26.

Dollar Limit: $3,500.

Where to Sue: Where defendant resides. Automobile accident cases: where occurred. Corporation resides where it has office, resident agent or place of business.

Service: First class mail, sheriff, or court-approved adult.

Hearing Date: Set by court.

Attorneys: Not allowed; required for corporations.

Transfer: By either side on jury demand or if defendant counterclaims for more than $3,500, case tried under regular civil procedure of County Court.

Appeals: By either side for new trial; to regular division of County Court within 20 days.

Special Provisions: No cases involving ownership of real estate. No jury trial. No pretrial attachments or garnishments. Court may order installment payments.

Mississippi   No small claims procedure (justice court)

Statutes: Mississippi Code Annotated 1972 (amendments to 1989), Title 11, Ch. 9, Sections 101–143.

Dollar Limit: $1,000.

Where to Sue: Where defendant resides. Nonresident defendants: where breach or injury occurred.

Service: Sheriff or constable.

Hearing Date: Set by court.

Attorneys: Allowed.

Transfer: No provision.

Appeals: By either side for new trial; to Circuit Court within 10 days.

Special Provisions: Jury trial available.

Missouri Small Claims (Circuit Court)

Statutes: Vernon's Annotated Missouri Statutes 1987 (amendments to 1989), Sections 482.300–365; Missouri Rules of Court, Rules of Practice and Procedure in Small Claims Court, Rules 140–155.

Dollar Limit: $1,500.

Where to Sue: Where defendant resides, where breach or injury occurred or where plaintiff resides and defendant is found. Corporation resides where it has office or agent.

Service: Certified mail.

Hearing Date: Set by court.

Attorneys: Allowed.

Transfer: If defendant files compulsory counterclaim for more than $1,000, case tried under regular civil procedure of court, unless both sides agree not to transfer case.

Appeals: By either side for new trial; to regular Circuit Court judge within 10 days.

Special Provisions: No discovery. No jury trial. Right to sue may not be transferred. Limit of 6 claims a year per plaintiff.

Montana Small Claims (Justice or District Court)

Statutes: Montana Code Annotated 1987 (amendments to 1986), Title 25, Ch. 35, Sections 501–807; Title 25, Ch. 34, Sections 101–404.

Dollar Limit: $2,500.

Where to Sue: Where defendant resides. Contracts: where performance expected.

Service: Sheriff or constable.

Hearing Date: District court: 10–30 days from filing of claim. Justice Court: 10–40 days.

Attorneys: Not allowed, unless all sides represented by attorneys.

Transfer: District Court: no provision. Justice Court: if defendant files notice within 10 days of receipt of complaint, case tried under regular civil procedure of court.

Appeals: District Court: by either side for new trial; to regular District Court procedure within 10 days. Justice Court: By either side for review of law, not facts; to District Court within 10 days.

Special Provisions: Jury trial available to defendant unless counterclaim filed. Right to sue may not be transferred. No personal injury or property damage cases. Limit of 10 claims a year per plaintiff.

Nebraska   Small Claims (County Court)
Statutes: Revised Statutes of Nebraska 1943 (amendments to 1988), Title 24, Sections 521–527.
Dollar Limit: $1,500.
Where to Sue: Where defendant or agent resides or does business or where breach or injury occurred. Corporation resides where it does business or has agent.
Service: Certified mail or sheriff.
Hearing Date: Set by court.
Attorneys: Not allowed.
Transfer: If defendant requests jury trial or counterclaim for more than $1,500, case tried under regular civil procedure of court.
Appeals: By either side for new trial; to District Court within 30 days.
Special Provisions: Equitable relief available. Right to sue may not be transferred. Limit of 2 claims a week up to 10 claims a year per plaintiff.

Nevada   Small Claims (Justice Court)
Statutes: Nevada Revised Statutes Annotated 1986 (amendments to 1989), Title 6, Sections 73.010–060; Justice Court Rules of Civil Procedure, Ch. XII, Rules 88–100.
Dollar Limit: $2,500.
Where to Sue: Where defendant resides. Corporation resides where it does business or maintains an office.
Service: Certified or registered mail, sheriff, constable or court-approved adult.
Hearing Date: Within 90 days from service.
Attorneys: Allowed.
Transfer: No provision.
Appeals: By either side for review of law, not facts; to District Court within 5 days.
Special Provisions: No equitable relief.

New Hampshire   Small Claims (District or Municipal Court)
Statutes: New Hampshire Revised Statutes Annotated 1983 (amendments to 1988), Sections 503:1–10.
Dollar Limit: $2,500.
Where to Sue: Where plaintiff or defendant resides. Nonresident defendants: where breach or injury occurred.

Service: Certified mail, sheriff or constable.

Hearing Date: At least 14 days from service.

Attorneys: Allowed.

Transfer: If either party requests jury trial and claim exceeds $500 or if defendant counterclaims for more than $2,500, case tried in Superior Court.

Appeals: By either side for review of law, not facts; to Supreme Court within 30 days.

Special Provisions: No cases involving ownership of real estate. No jury trial.

New Jersey   Division of Small Claims (County District Court)

Statutes: New Jersey Statutes Annotated 1987 (amendments to 1989), Title 2A, Ch. 6, Sections 41–44; County District Court Civil Practice Rules, Rule 6:11.

Dollar Limit: $1,000.

Where to Sue: Where defendant resides. Nonresident defendants: where breach or injury occurred.

Service: Certified mail, sheriff, sergeant at arms or court-approved adult.

Hearing Date: Set by court.

Attorneys: Allowed.

Transfer: If defendant requests jury trial or counterclaims for more than $1,000, case tried under regular civil procedure of Civil Part.

Appeals: By either side for review of law, not facts; to Appellate Division of Superior Court within 45 days.

Special Provisions: Only contract, property damage caused by motor vehicles and landlord-tenant security deposit cases. Right to sue may not be transferred.

New Mexico   No small claims procedure (Metropolitan Court or Magistrate Court)

Statutes: New Mexico Statutes 1978 (amendments to 1989), Sections 34.8A.1–9 and 35.3.3–6.

Dollar Limit: $5,000.

Where to Sue: Where plaintiff or defendant resides or where breach or injury occurred. Recovery of property: where property is. Corporation resides where it has an office or agent.

Service: Sheriff or court-approved adult.

Hearing Date: Set by court.

Attorneys: Allowed; required for corporations.

Transfer: No provision.

Appeals: By either side for review of law, not facts; to District Court within 15 days.
Special Provisions: Jury trial available.

New York   Small Claims (New York City: Civil Court; Nassau, Suffolk Counties: District Court, except 1st District; other cities: City Court; rural: Justice Court)
Statutes: Consolidated Laws of New York Annotated 1969 (amendments to 1989), Uniform District Court Act, Sections 1801–1814; Uniform Justice Court Act, Sections 1801–1814; N.Y.C. Civil Court Act, Sections 1801–1814; Civil Practice Law and Rules, Section 321(a); N.Y.C. Civil Court Rule 2900.33.
Dollar Limit: $2,000.
Where to Sue: Where defendant resides, is employed or maintains a business office.
Service: Certified or registered mail or court-approved adult.
Hearing Date: Set by court.
Attorneys: Allowed; required for most corporations.
Transfer: Within court's discretion to appropriate court.
Appeals: By defendant only for review of law, not facts, or by plaintiff if "substantial justice" was not done; to County Court or Appellate Terms within 30 days.
Special Provisions: No equitable relief. Nonappealable arbitration available. Corporations and partnerships may not sue. Right to sue may not be transferred. Jury trial available to defendant. Business judgment debtors must pay within 35 days or $100 may be added to judgment. Businesses that fail to pay judgments may face triple damages. No counterclaims allowed in small claims unless within the dollar limit.

North Carolina   Small Claims (Magistrate Court)
Statutes: General Statutes of North Carolina 1986 (amendments to 1988), Ch. 7A, Sections 210–232.
Dollar Limit: $2,000.
Where to Sue: Where defendant resides. Corporation resides where it has place of business.
Service: Certified or registered mail, sheriff or court-approved adult.
Hearing Date: Within 30 days of filing claim.
Attorneys: Allowed.
Transfer: No provision.

Appeals: By either side for new trial; to District Court within 10 days.

Special Provisions: No equitable relief except enforcement of liens. No counterclaims allowed in small claims unless within the dollar limit.

North Dakota Small Claims (County Court)

Statutes: North Dakota Century Code Annotated 1974 (amendments to 1989), Title 27, Sections 08.1–01 to 1–08.

Dollar Limit: $2,000.

Where to Sue: Where defendant resides. Corporation resides where it does business or where breach or injury occurred.

Service: Certified mail or court-approved adult.

Hearing Date: 10–30 days from service.

Attorneys: Allowed.

Transfer: If defendant requests, case tried under regular civil procedure of court.

Appeals: Not allowed.

Special Provisions: No equitable relief except to cancel agreements obtained by fraud or misrepresentation. No jury trial. Right to sue may not be transferred. No prejudgment attachment. Plaintiff's withdrawal of case results in dismissal with prejudice.

Ohio Small Claims Division (County or Municipal Court)

Statutes: Page's Ohio Revised Code Annotated 1983 (amendments to 1989), Title 19, Ch. 1925, Sections .01–.17; Ohio Rules of Civil Procedure.

Dollar Limit: $1,000.

Where to Sue: Where defendant resides, has a place of business or where breach or injury occurred. Nonresident defendants: where plaintiff resides. Corporation resides where it has principal place of business or an agent.

Service: Certified mail, sheriff, bailiff or court-approved adult.

Hearing Date: 15–40 days from filing of complaint.

Attorneys: Allowed. A corporation may proceed through an officer or employee, but may not cross-examine, argue or advocate except through attorney.

Transfer: If either side requests, if defendant counterclaims for more than $1,500, or at court's discretion, case tried under regular civil procedure of appropriate court.

Appeals: By either side for review of law, not facts; to Court of Appeals within 30 days.

Special Provisions: No equitable relief. No jury trial. No discovery. No libel or slander cases. Right to sue may not be transferred. Limit of 24 claims a year per plaintiff. Court may order arbitration. Mediation is available in some jursidictions.

Oklahoma   Small Claims Division (District Court)
Statutes: Oklahoma Statutes Annotated 1980 (amendments to 1989), Title 12, Sections 1751–1771.
Dollar Limit: $2,500.
Where to Sue: Where defendant resides, debt arose or contract signed. Damage to land or buildings: where property is. Corporations: where principal office is, where officer resides, where any codefendant is sued or where injury occurred. Nonresident corporations: where property or debts are due, where agent is found, where any codefendant is sued, where injury occurred or where plaintiff resides.
Service: Certified mail, sheriff or court-approved adult.
Hearing Date: 10–30 days from filing of complaint.
Attorneys: Allowed.
Transfer: If defendant counterclaims for more than $2,500 or if court grants defendant's request, case tried under regular civil procedure of court.
Appeals: By either side for review of law, not facts; to Supreme Court within 30 days.
Special Provisions: Cases only to recover money, personal property or debt-payment distribution to several creditors. No libel or slander cases. Jury trial available. Collection agents may not sue. Right to sue may not be transferred.

Oregon   Small Claims (District or Justice Court)
Statutes: Oregon Revised Statutes 1988 (amendments to 1989), Sections 46.010–760; Sections 55.011–140.
Dollar Limit: $2,500.
Where to Sue: Where defendant resides or is found or where injury occurred. Contracts: where performance expected.
Service: Certified mail, sheriff, constable or court-approved adult.
Hearing Date: District Court: set by court. Justice Court: 5–10 days from service.
Attorneys: Not allowed unless court consents.
Transfer: If defendant counterclaims for more than $2,500 or either side requests jury trial, case goes to mandatory nonbinding arbitration in District Court. If still dissatisfied, case tried in District Court.

Appeals: District Court: not allowed. Justice Court: by defendant or counterdefendant for new trial; to circuit court within 10 days.

Special Provisions: Plaintiff must attest to good faith efforts to collect before filing claim. In District Court, defendant must answer within 14 days or lose by default. Cases may be referred to mediation or arbitration.

Pennsylvania No small claims procedure (Philadelphia: Municipal Court; elsewhere: District Justice Court)

Statutes: Pennsylvania Statutes Annotated 1981 (amendments to 1989), Title 42, Sections 1511–1516; Rules of Civil Procedure Governing District Justices, Rules 201–325; Philadelphia Municipal Rules of Civil Practice, Rules 101–134.

Dollar Limit: Municipal Court: $5,000; District Justice Court: $4,000.

Where to Sue: Where defendant resides or is found or where breach or injury occurred. Corporation resides where it has principal place of business.

Service: Certified or registered mail, sheriff or court-approved adult.

Hearing Date: Municipal Court: set by court. District Justice Court: 12–60 days from service.

Attorneys: Allowed; required for corporations, except when corporation is defendant and claim is for less than $1,000.

Transfer: Municipal Court: if defendant counterclaims for more than $5,000, case tried in Court of Common Pleas. District Justice Court: no provision.

Appeals: By either side for new trial; to court of common pleas within 30 days.

Special Provisions: District Justice Court: no cases involving ownership of real estate; court may order installment payments; court may order arbitration. Municipal Court: no jury trial. If defendant appeals, any part of plaintiff's previously waived claim for more than $5,000 may be considered on appeal.

Puerto Rico No small claims procedure (District Court)

Statutes: Laws of Puerto Rico Annotated 1983 (amendments to 1988), Title 32, Appendix III, Rule 60.

Dollar Limit: $2,000.

Where to Sue: Where defendant resides. Corporation resides where it does business or where obligation incurred.

Service: By clerk's written notice.

Hearing Date: Set by court.

Attorneys: Allowed.

Transfer: No provision.

Appeals: By either side for review of law, not facts; to Superior Court within 10 days.

Special Provisions: No personal injury or property damage cases. Defendant must file written answer at or before the hearing. Court may order installment payments. All pleadings must be in Spanish, or Spanish translations must be provided.

Rhode Island   Small Claims (District Court)

Statutes: General Laws of Rhode Island 1985 (amendments to 1988), Title 10, Ch. 16, Sections 1–16.

Dollar Limit: $1,500.

Where to Sue: Where either side resides. Corporation resides where it does business.

Service: Certified or registered mail (binding on defendant who refuses to accept), sheriff, deputy, constable or court-approved adult.

Hearing Date: Set by court.

Attorneys: Allowed; required for corporations, except close and family corporations with less than $1 million in assets.

Transfer: If defendant counterclaims for more than $1,500, case tried under regular civil procedure of District Court.

Appeals: By defendant only for new trial; to Superior Court within 2 days.

Special Provisions: No personal injury or property damage cases. Court may order installment payments.

South Carolina   No small claims procedure (Magistrate Court)

Statutes: Code of Laws of South Carolina 1976 (amendments to 1989), Title 22, Ch. 3, Sections 10–320; Administrative and Procedural Rules for Magistrate's Court, Rules 1–19.

Dollar Limit: $2,500; none in landlord-tenant cases.

Where to Sue: Where defendant resides. Nonresident defendants: where plaintiff designates. To recover personal property: where property is. Corporation resides where it does business.

Service: Certified or registered mail, sheriff, deputy, attorney in case or court-approved disinterested adult.

Hearing Date: Set by court.

Attorneys: Allowed.

Transfer: If defendant counterclaims for more than $2,500, case tried under regular civil procedure of appropriate court.

Appeals: By either side for review of law, not facts; to Circuit Court within 30 days.

Special Provisions: Jury trial available. Defendant must answer within 20 days (30 days if claim for less than $25) or lose by default. No cases for more than $100 against the state and no cases involving ownership of real estate.

South Dakota Small Claims Division (Circuit or Magistrate Court)

Statutes: South Dakota Compiled Laws Annotated 1984 (amendments to 1989), Title 15, Ch. 39, Sections 45–78.

Dollar Limit: $2,000.

Where to Sue: Where defendant resides or injury occurred. Corporation resides where it does business.

Service: Certified or registered mail; if that fails, sheriff or court-approved adult.

Hearing Date: Set by court.

Attorneys: Allowed.

Transfer: If defendant requests jury trial at least 2 days before hearing, to regular civil procedure of appropriate court.

Appeals: Not allowed.

Special Provisions: No libel or slander cases. Court may order installment payments. Defendant must answer at least 2 days before hearing or lose by default.

Tennessee No small claims procedure (Court of General Sessions or Justice Court)

Statutes: Tennessee Code Annotated 1980 (amendments to 1988), Title 16, Ch. 15, Sections 501–713.

Dollar Limit: $10,000; in counties of more than 700,000 population, $15,000. No limit in eviction cases or to recover specific personal property, except $25,000 limit for alternative money judgments in personal property cases in counties of less than 700,000 population.

Where to Sue: Where defendant resides or is found or where injury occurred. To recover personal property: where property is. Corporation resides where it maintains an office.

Service: Certified mail, sheriff, deputy or constable.

Hearing Date: Set by court.

Attorneys: Allowed.

Transfer: No provision.

Appeals: By either side for new trial; to Circuit Court within 10 days.

Special Provisions: Equitable relief limited to restraining orders. No jury trial. No formal pleadings required.

Texas   Small Claims (Justice Court)
Statutes: Texas Code Annotated 1988 (amendments to 1989), Government Code, Sections 28.001–055; Texas Rules of Civil Procedure.
Dollar Limit: $2,500.
Where to Sue: Where defendant resides. Contracts: where performance expected.
Service: Certified mail, sheriff, constable or court-approved adult.
Hearing Date: Set by court.
Attorneys: Allowed.
Transfer: No provision.
Appeals: By either side for claims of more than $20; to Constitutional County Court or County Court at law within 10 days.
Special Provisions: No equitable relief. Jury trial available if requested at least 1 day before trial. Right to sue may not be transferred. Collection agents and commercial lenders may not sue.

Utah   Small Claims (Circuit or Justice Court)
Statutes: Utah Code Annotated 1953 (amendments to 1989), Sections 78.6.1–15.
Dollar Limit: $1,000.
Where to Sue: Where defendant resides or where breach or injury occurred.
Service: Sheriff, deputy, constable or disinterested adult.
Hearing Date: Set by court.
Attorneys: Allowed.
Transfer: No provision.
Appeals: By either side for new trial; to Circuit Court within 10 days.
Special Provisions: No jury trial. Right to sue may not be transferred. Evening sessions available.

Vermont   Small Claims (District Court)
Statutes: Vermont Statutes Annotated 1973 (amendments to 1989), Title 12, Sections 405, 5531–5538.
Dollar Limit: $2,000.
Where to Sue: Where either side resides or where breach or injury occurred.
Service: First-class mail or sheriff.
Hearing Date: Set by court.
Attorneys: Allowed.
Transfer: If defendant requests jury trial, to regular civil procedure of court.
Appeals: By either side for review of law, not facts; to Superior Court within 30 days.

Special Provisions: No equitable relief. Defendant must file written answer within 20 days or lose by default. Defendant may counter-claim (not involving third parties outside court's jurisdiction) for more than $2,000, but court may not award more than $2,000; defendant may later sue in separate action for the difference. Defendant may request jury trial. No libel or slander cases.

Virgin Islands Small Claims (Territorial Court)
Statutes: Virgin Islands Code Annotated 1979 (amendments to 1989), Title 4, Ch. 3, Sections 32–33; Title 5, Ch. 7, Sections 111–112; Title 5, Ch. 9, Sections 141–142 and Appendices IV and VII.
Dollar Limit: $2,000.
Where to Sue: Where defendant resides or where breach or injury occurred.
Service: Registered mail, marshal or court-approved adult.
Hearing Date: 5–15 days from service.
Attorneys: Not allowed.
Transfer: If either side requests jury trial or defendant counter-claims for more than $2,000 and court permits, case tried under regular civil procedure of court.
Appeals: By either side for review of law, not facts; to United States District Court within 10 days.
Special Provisions: Pretrial conciliation encouraged. Court may order installment payments. No jury trial.

Virginia No small claims procedure (General District Court)
Statutes: Code of Virginia 1982 (amendments to 1989), Sections 16.1.76–113 and 122.1–122.7.
Dollar Limit: $7,000.
Where to Sue: Where defendant resides, is employed or regularly transacts business, or where breach or injury occurred. To recover property: where property is.
Service: Sheriff or court-approved adult.
Hearing Date: Set by court.
Attorneys: Allowed.
Transfer: If defendant counterclaims for more than $1,000 and requests transfer, case tried in Circuit Court.
Appeals: By either side for new trial on claims more than $50; to Circuit Court within 10 days.
Special Provisions: The General District Court in Fairfax has a small claims division, through 1990. It will probably be continued. Any Virginia resident may file a claim. Court operates on Fridays, has a $1,000 limit and does not allow attorneys.

Washington   Small Claims Department (District Court)
Statutes: Revised Code of Washington Annotated 1962 (amendments to 1989), Title 12, Sections 40.010–120.
Dollar Limit: $2,000.
Where to Sue: Where defendant resides. Corporation resides where it does business or has an office.
Service: Certified or registered mail, sheriff, deputy, constable or disinterested adult.
Hearing Date: Set by court.
Attorneys: Not allowed unless court consents.
Transfer: If plaintiff is a corporation represented by an attorney and defendant requests transfer, case tried under regular civil procedure of court.
Appeals: By side that requests small claims court jurisdiction when the amount is more than $1,000 or by defendant when the amount is more than $100; for new trial, to Superior Court within 14 days.
Special Provisions: No equitable relief. Counterclaims for more than $2,000 must be filed separately in appropriate court.

West Virginia   No small claims procedure (Magistrate Court)
Statutes: West Virginia Code 1986 (amendments to 1989), Ch. 50, Sections 1.1–6.3; Ch. 56, Sections 1.1, 1.2.
Dollar Limit: $3,000.
Where to Sue: Where defendant resides or where injury occurred. Contracts: where breach occurred. Property insurance claims: where property is. Nonresident defendants: where plaintiff resides or where defendant has property or debts due. Corporation resides where it has principal office or where chief officer resides. Nonresident U.S. corporate defendants: where corporation does business or where plaintiff resides.
Service: Sheriff; if that fails, any credible disinterested adult or attorney in case.
Hearing Date: Defendant has 20 days to appear (5 days in eviction cases). Trial date set after defendant notifies court of intention to defend against claim.
Attorneys: Allowed; required for collection agents.
Transfer: Claims less than $300: if both sides consent, case tried in Circuit Court. Claims more than $300: if either side requests, case tried in Circuit Court.
Appeals: By either side for new trial; to circuit court within 20 days.
Special Provisions: No equitable relief. Jury trial available on claim of $20. Defendant must answer within 20 days or lose by default. No libel or slander, ownership of real estate, foreclosure of real

estate liens, false imprisonment or eminent domain cases. Claims against the state must be brought in the Court of Claims at the State Capitol.

Wisconsin   Small Claims (Circuit Court)
Statutes: Wisconsin Statutes Annotated 1981 (amendments to 1989), Sections 799.01–45.
Dollar Limit: $2,000; none in eviction cases.
Where to Sue: Where defendant resides or does substantial business or where breach or injury occurred. Consumer credit claims: where customer resides, collateral is or document signed. Corporation resides where it has principal office or where it does business.
Service: Certified or registered mail, any disinterested adult resident.
Hearing Date: 8–30 days after summons issued (5–30 days in eviction cases).
Attorneys: Allowed; required for assignees.
Transfer: If either side requests jury trial or if defendant files compulsory counterclaim for more than $2,000, case tried under regular civil procedure of court.
Appeals: By either side for review of law, not facts; to Court of Appeals within 45 days (15 days in eviction cases).
Special Provisions: Prevailing party may be awarded attorney fees up to $100 on judgments more than $1,000. Jury trial available. Evening and Saturday sessions available.

Wyoming   Small Claims (County or Justice of the Peace Court)
Statutes: Wyoming Statutes Annotated 1977 (amendments to 1989), Sections 1.5.101–108 and 1.21.201–205; Rules of Civil Procedure for Justice of the Peace Courts, Rules 1–8.
Dollar Limit: $2,000.
Where to Sue: Where defendant resides or is found. Corporation resides where it has principal place of business. Nonresident defendants: where breach or injury occurred.
Service: Certified or registered mail, sheriff, deputy, deputized process server or court-approved adult.
Hearing Date: 3–12 days from service.
Attorneys: Allowed.
Transfer: No provision.
Appeals: By either side for review of law, not facts; to District Court within 10 days.
Special Provisions: Jury trial available. No formal pleadings required.

ALTERNATIVE RESOURCES

$\mathbf{A}$s discussed in Chapter 2, small claims courts may not accurately address or provide the best solution to every small claims dispute that occurs. This appendix lists a variety of out-of-court alternatives for resolving disputes. Some of the information in this and later appendices is excerpted from the 1990 edition of the *Consumer's Resource Handbook,* published by the U.S. Office of Consumer Affairs.

CONSUMER INFORMATION

Consumer Information Center
Pueblo, CO 81009

PRIVATE CONSUMER ACTION AGENCIES (CAAs)

Consumer Federation of America
1424 16th St. NW, Suite 604
Washington, DC 20036
(202) 387-6121

National Consumers League
815 15th St. NW, Suite 516
Washington, DC 20005
(202) 639-8140

Call for Action National Center
3400 Idaho Ave. NW
Washington, DC 20016
(202) 537-0585

CONSUMER ACTION PANELS (CAPs)

Automotive Consumer Action
Program (AUTOCAP)
8400 Westpark Dr.
McLean, VA 22102
(703) 821-7144

Major Appliance Consumer
Action Panel (MACAP)
20 N. Wacker Dr.
Chicago, IL 60606
(312) 984-5858

TRADE ASSOCIATIONS

American Apparel
  Manufacturers Association
2500 Wilson Blvd., Suite 301
Arlington, VA 22201
(703) 524-1864

American Automobile
  Association
8111 Gatehouse Rd., Suite 535
Falls Church, VA 22047
(703) 222-6446

American Collectors
  Association
4040 W. 70th St.
Minneapolis, MN 55435
(612) 926-6547

American Council of Life
  Insurance
1001 Pennsylvania Ave. NW
Washington, DC 20004-2599
(Written inquiries only)

American Health Care
  Association
1201 L St. NW
Washington, DC 20005
(202) 842-4444

American Hotel and Motel
  Association
1201 New York Ave., Suite 600
Washington, DC 20005
(Written inquiries only)

American Society of Travel
  Agents, Inc.
P.O. Box 23992
Washington, DC 20026
(703) 739-2782

Better Hearing Institute
P.O. Box 1840
Washington, DC 20013
(703) 642-0580
(800) Ear-Well (toll free
  nationwide)

Blue Cross/Blue Shield
  Association
655 15th St. NW, Suite 350
Washington, DC 20005
(202) 626-4780

Carpet and Rug Institute
1155 Connecticut Ave., Suite
  500
Washington, DC 20036
(Written inquiries only)

Cemetery Consumer Service
  Council
P.O. Box 3574
Washington, DC 20007
(703) 379-6426
(Handles complaints about
  cemetery practices)

Direct Mail Marketing
  Association
6 E. 43rd St.
New York, NY 10017
(Written inquiries only;
  complaints about junk mail)

Electronic Industries
  Association
2001 Eye St. NW
Washington, DC 20006
(202) 457-4900

Funeral Service Consumer
Arbitration Program
11121 W. Oklahoma Ave.
Milwaukee, WI 53227
(414) 541-2500
(Offered by the National
Funeral Directors
Association)

International Fabricare
Institute
12251 Tech Rd.
Silver Spring, MD 20904
(301) 622-1900
(Dry-cleaning complaints)

Mail Order Action Line
6 E. 43rd St.
New York, NY 10017
(Written inquiries only;
complaints about mail-order
and telephone solicitation
companies)

Mail Preference Service
P.O. Box 3861
Grand Central Station
New York, NY 10163
(Written inquiries only; Will
remove your name from a
direct-mail list)

National Association of Home
Builders
15th and M Sts. NW
Washington, DC 20005
(202) 822-0409
(Coordinates "Home Owners
Warranty" [HOW] program)

National Association of
Personnel Consultants
3133 Mt. Vernon Ave.
Alexandria, VA 22303
(703) 684-0180

(Arbitrates consumer
complaints with
employment agencies,
recruiting firms and
temporary help services)

National Association of
Professional Insurance
Agents
400 N. Washington St.
Alexandria, VA 22314
(703) 836-9340

National Association of
Securities Dealers
33 Whitehall St., 10th Floor
New York, NY 10004
(212) 858-4000
(Operates arbitration program
for conflicts between
investors and broker
members)

National Foundation for
Consumer Credit
8701 Georgia Ave., Suite 507
Silver Spring, MD 20910
(301) 589-5600

National Home Study Council
1601 18th St. NW
Washington, DC 20009
(Written inquiries only:
information about home
study correspondence
schools)

Pharmaceutical Manufacturers
Association
1100 15th St. NW, Suite 900
Washington, DC 20005
(202) 835-3468

Toy Manufacturers of America
200 5th Ave.

New York, NY 10010
(212) 675-1141

ALTERNATIVE DISPUTE RESOLUTION RESOURCES

American Arbitration
  Association (National Office)
140 W. 51st St., 10th Floor
New York, NY 10020
(212) 661-4451

American Bar Association
Standing Committee on
  Dispute Resolution
1800 M St. NW
Washington, DC 20036
(202) 331-2258

Better Business Bureau
AUTOLINE
4200 Wilson Blvd., Suite 800
Arlington, VA 22203
(703) 276-0100

Center for Public Resources
366 Madison Ave.
New York, NY 10017
(212) 949-6490

Federal Mediation and
  Conciliation Service
2100 K St. NW
Washington, DC 20037
(202) 543-5320

Society of Professionals in
  Dispute Resolution
1730 Rhode Island Ave. NW,
  Suite 909
Washington, DC 20036
(202) 833-2188

BETTER BUSINESS BUREAUS (BBBS)

Better Business Bureaus are nonprofit organizations sponsored by local businesses. They offer a variety of consumer services. For example, they can provide consumer education materials, answer consumer questions, mediate and arbitrate complaints, and provide general information on consumer complaint records of companies. This list includes the local BBBs in the United States. The national headquarters can give you the addresses for BBBs in Canada and Israel.

National Headquarters

Council of Better Business
Bureaus
4200 Wilson Blvd.
Arlington, VA 22203
(703) 276-0100

Local Bureaus

Alabama

1214 S. 20th St.
Birmingham, AL 35205
(205) 558-2222

P.O. Box 383
Huntsville, AL 35804
(205) 533-1640

707 Van Antwerp Bldg.
Mobile, AL 36602
(205) 433-5494/5495

Commerce St., Suite 810
Montgomery, AL 36104
(205) 262-5606

Alaska

3380 C St., Suite 100
Anchorage, AK 99503
(907) 562-0704

Arizona

4428 N. 12th St.
Phoenix, AZ 85014
(602) 264-1721

50 W. Drachman St., Suite 103
Tucson, AZ 85705
(602) 622-7651 (inquiries)
(602) 622-7654 (complaints)

Arkansas

1415 S. University Ave.
Little Rock, AR 72204
(501) 664-7274

California

705—18th St.
Bakersfield, CA 93301
(805) 322-2074

P.O. Box 970
Colton, CA 92324
(714) 825-7280

6101 Ball Rd., Suite 309
Cypress, CA 90630
(714) 527-0680

5070 N. Sixth, Suite 176
Fresno, CA 93710
(209) 222-8111

510—16th St., Suite 550
Oakland, CA 94612
(415) 839-5900

400 S St.
Sacramento, CA 95814
(916) 443-6843

525 B St., Suite 301
San Diego, CA 92101-4408
(619) 234-0966

33 New Montgomery St. Tower
San Francisco, CA 94105
(415) 243-9999

1505 Meridian Ave.
San Jose, CA 95125
(408) 978-8700

P.O. Box 294
San Mateo, CA 94401
(415) 347-1251

P.O. Box 746
Santa Barbara, CA 93102
(805) 963-8657

1111 North Center St.
Stockton, CA 95202
(209) 948-4880, 4881

Colorado

P.O. Box 7970
Colorado Springs, CO 80933
(719) 636-1155

1780 S. Bellaire, Suite 700
Denver, CO 80222
(303) 758-2100 (inquiries)
(303) 758-2212 (complaints)

1730 S. College Ave., #303
Fort Collins, CO 80525
(303) 484-1348

432 Broadway
Pueblo, CO 81004
(719) 542-6464

Connecticut

2345 Black Rock Tpk.
Fairfield, CT 06430
(203) 374-6161

2080 Silas Deane Hwy.
Rocky Hill, CT 06067-2311
(203) 529-3575

100 S. Turnpike Rd.
Wallingford, CT 06492
(203) 269-2700 (inquiries)
(203) 269-4457 (complaints)

Delaware

P.O. Box 300
Milford, DE 19963
(302) 422-6300 (Kent)
(302) 856-6969 (Sussex)

P.O. Box 5361
Wilmington, DE 19808
(302) 996-9200

District of Columbia

1012 14th St. NW
Washington, DC 20005
(202) 393-8000

Florida

13770—58th St. N., #309
Clearwater, FL 33520
(813) 535-5522

2976-E Cleveland Ave.
Fort Myers, FL 33901
(813) 334-7331/7152
(813) 597-1322 (Naples)
(813) 743-2279 (Port Charlotte)

3100 University Blvd. S., #23
Jacksonville, FL 32216
(904) 721-2288

2605 Maitland Center Pkwy.
Maitland, FL 32751-7147
(407) 660-9500

16291 N.W. 57th Ave.
Miami, FL 33014-6709
(305) 625-0307 (inquiries for
Dade County)
(305) 625-1302 (complaints for
Dade County)
(305) 524-2803 (inquiries for
Broward County)
(305) 527-1643 (complaints for
Broward County)

250 School Rd., Suite 11-W
New Port Richey, FL 34652
(813) 842-5459

P.O. Box 1511
Pensacola, FL 32597-1511
(904) 433-6111

1950 Port St. Lucie Blvd., #211
Port St. Lucie, FL 34952
(407) 878-2010/337-2083

1111 N. Westshore Blvd., Suite
207
Tampa, FL 33607
(813) 875-6200

2247 Palm Beach Lakes Blvd.,
#211
West Palm Beach, FL 33409-3408
(407) 686-2200

Georgia

1319-B Dawson Road
Albany, GA 31707
(912) 883-0744

100 Edgewood Ave.,
Suite 1012
Atlanta, GA 30303
(404) 688-4910

P.O. Box 2085
Augusta, GA 30903
(404) 722-1574

P.O. Box 2587
Columbus, GA 31902
(404) 324-0712 (inquiries)
(404) 324-0713 (complaints)

6606 Abercorn St., Suite 108-C
Savannah, GA 31416
(912) 354-7521

Hawaii

1600 Kapiolani Blvd., Suite 704
Honolulu, HI 96814
(808) 942-2355

Idaho

409 W. Jefferson
Boise, ID 83702
(208) 342-4649
(208) 467-5547

545 Shoup, Suite 210
Idaho Falls, ID 83402
(208) 523-9754

Illinois

211 W. Wacker Dr.
Chicago, IL 60606
(312) 444-1188 (inquiries)
(312) 346-3313 (complaints)

109 S.W. Jefferson St., #305
Peoria, IL 61602
(309) 673-5194

515 N. Court St.
Rockford, IL 61110
(815) 963-BBB2

Indiana

P.O. Box 405
Elkhart, IN 46515
(219) 262-8996

119 S.E. Fourth St.
Evansville, IN 47708
(812) 422-6879

1203 Webster St.
Fort Wayne, IN 46802
(219) 423-4433

4231 Cleveland St.
Gary, IN 46408
(219)   980-1511/769-8053/926-
5669

Victoria Centre
22 East Washington St.
Indianapolis, IN 46204
(317) 637-0197

320 S. Washington St., #101
Marion, IN 46952
(317) 668-8954/8955

Whitinger Building, Room 150
Muncie, IN 47306
(317) 285-5668

509—85 U.S. #33 North
South Bend, IN 46637
(219) 277-9121

Iowa

2435 Kimberly Road, #110 North
Bettendorf, IA 52722
(319) 355-6344

1500 Second Avenue SE, #212
Cedar Rapids, IA 52403
(319) 366-5401

615 Insurance Exchange Bldg.
Des Moines, IA 50309
(515) 243-8137

318 Badgerow Bldg.
Siouxland, IA 51101
(712) 252-4501

Kansas

501 Jefferson, Suite 24
Topeka, KS 66607
(913) 232-0455

300 Kaufman Bldg.
Wichita, KS 67202
(316) 263-3146

Kentucky

154 Patchen Dr., Suite 90
Lexington, KY 40502
(606) 268-4128

844 Fourth St.
Louisville, KY 40203
(502) 583-6546

Louisiana

1605 Murray St., Suite 117
Alexandria, LA 71301
(318) 473-4494

2055 Wooddale Blvd.
Baton Rouge, LA 70806
(504) 926-3010

300 Bond St.
Houma, LA 70361
(504) 868-3456

P.O. Box 30297
Lafayette, LA 70593
(318) 234-8341

P.O. Box 1681
Lake Charles, LA 70602
(318) 433-1633

141 De Siard St., Suite 300
Monroe, LA 71201
(318) 387-4600, 4601

1539 Jackson Ave.
New Orleans, LA 70130
(504) 581-6222

1401 N. Market St.
Shreveport, LA 71101
(318) 221-8352

Maine

812 Stevens Ave.
Portland, ME 04103
(207) 878-2715

Maryland

2100 Huntingdon Ave.
Baltimore, MD 21211-3215
(301) 347-3990

Massachusetts

Eight Winter St.
Boston, MA 02108
(617) 482-9151 (inquiries)
(617) 482-9190 (complaints)

One Kendall St., Suite 307
Framingham, MA 01701
(508) 872-5585

78 North St., Suite 1
Hyannis, MA 02601
(508) 771-3022

316 Essex St.
Lawrence, MA 01840
(508) 687-7666

106 State Rd., Suite 4
North Dartmouth, MA 02747
(508) 999-6060

293 Bridge St., Suite 324
Springfield, MA 01103
(413) 734-3114

P.O. Box 379
Worcester, MA 01601
(508) 755-2548

Michigan

150 Michigan Ave.
Detroit, MI 48226
(313) 962-7566 (inquiries)
(313) 962-6785 (complaints)

620 Trust Bldg.
Grand Rapids, MI 49503
(616) 774-8236

Minnesota

1745 University Ave.
St. Paul, MN 55104
(612) 646-7700

Mississippi

2917 W. Beach Blvd., #103
Biloxi, MS 39531
(601) 374-2222

105 Fifth St.
Columbus, MS 39701
(601) 327-8594

P.O. Box 390
Jackson, MS 39205-0390
(601) 948-8222

Missouri

306 E. 12th St., Suite 1024
Kansas City, MO 64106
(816) 421-7800

5100 Oakland, Suite 200
St. Louis, MO 63110
(314) 531-3300

205 Park Central East, #509
Springfield, MO 65806
(417) 862-9231

Nebraska

719 N. 48th St.
Lincoln, NE 68504
(402) 467-5261

1613 Farnam St.
Omaha, NE 68102
(402) 346-3033

Nevada

1022 E. Sahara Ave.
Las Vegas, NV 89104
(702) 735-6900/1969

P.O. Box 21269
Reno, NV 89505
(702) 322-0657

New Hampshire

410 S. Main St.
Concord, NH 03301
(603) 224-1991
(800) 852-3757 (toll free in NH)

New Jersey

34 Park Pl.
Newark, NJ 07102
(201) 642-INFO

Two Forest Ave.
Paramus, NJ 07652
(201) 845-4044

1721 Rte. #37 East
Toms River, NJ 08753
(201) 270-5577

1700   Whitehorse—Hamilton
    Square
Trenton, NJ 08690
(609) 588-0808 (Mercer County)
(201)   536-6306   (Monmouth
    County)
(201) 329-6855
(Middlesex, Somerset and Hunt-
    erdon counties)

New Mexico

4600-A Montgomery NE, #200
Albuquerque, NM 87109
(505) 884-0500
(800) 445-1461 (toll free in NM)

308 N. Locke
Farmington, NM 87401
(505) 326-6501

2407 W. Picacho, Suite B-2
Las Cruces, NM 88005
(505) 524-3130

1210 Luisa St., Suite 5
Santa Fe, NM 87502
(505) 988-3648

New York

346 Delaware Ave.
Buffalo, NY 14202
(716) 856-7180

266 Main St.
Farmingdale, NY 11735
(516) 420-0500

257 Park Ave. South
New York, NY 10010
(212) 533-6200

1122 Sibley Tower
Rochester, NY 14604
(716) 546-6776

100 University Bldg.
Syracuse, NY 13202
(315) 479-6635

120 E. Main St.
Wappinger Falls, NY 12590
(914) 297-6550

30 Glenn St.
White Plains, NY 10603
(914) 428-1230/1231

North Carolina

801 BBB&T Bldg.
Asheville, NC 28801
(704) 253-2392

1130 E. 3rd St., Suite 400
Charlotte, NC 28204
(704) 332-7151
(800) 532-0477 (toll free in NC)

3608 W. Friendly Ave.
Greensboro, NC 27410
(919) 852-4240/4241/4242

P.O. Box 1882
Hickory, NC 28603
(704) 464-0372

3120 Poplarwood Dr., Suite 101
Raleigh, NC 27604-1080
(919) 872-9240

2110 Cloverdale Ave., #2-B
Winston-Salem, NC 27103
(919) 725-8348

Ohio

P.O. Box 80596
Akron, OH 44308
(216) 253-4590

1434 Cleveland Ave. NW
Canton, OH 44703
(216) 454-9401

898 Walnut St.
Cincinnati, OH 45202
(513) 421-3015

2217 E. 9th St., Suite 200
Cleveland, OH 44115
(216) 241-7678

527 S. High St.
Columbus, OH 43215
(614) 221-6336

40 W. Fourth St., #1250, Suite 280
Dayton, OH 45402
(513) 222-5825
(800) 521-8357 (toll free in OH)

P.O. Box 269
Lima, OH 45802
(419) 223-7010

P.O. Box 1706
Mansfield, OH 44910
(419) 522-1700

425 Jefferson Ave., Suite 909
Toledo, OH 43604
(419) 241-6276

345 N. Market
Wooster, OH 44691
(216) 263-6444

P.O. Box 1495
Youngstown, OH 44501
(216) 744-3111

Oklahoma

17 S. Dewey
Oklahoma City, OK 73102
(405) 239-6860 (inquiries)
(405) 239-6081 (inquiries)
(405) 239-6083 (complaints)

6711 S. Yale, Suite 230
Tulsa, OK 71436
(918) 492-1266

Oregon

601 S.W. Alder St., Suite 615
Portland, OR 97205
(503) 226-3981

Pennsylvania

528 N. New St.
Bethlehem, PA 18018
(215) 866-8780

6 Marion Court
Lancaster, PA 17602
(717) 291-1151
(717) 232-2800 (Harrisburg)
(717) 846-2700 (York County)

P.O. Box 2297
Philadelphia, PA 19103
(215) 496-1000

610 Smithfield St.
Pittsburgh, PA 15222
(412) 456-2700

P.O. Box 993
Scranton, PA 18501
(717) 342-9129

Puerto Rico

G.P.O. Box 70212
San Juan, PR 00936
(809) 756-5400

Rhode Island

Bureau Park
P.O. Box 1300
Warwick, RI 02887-1300
(401) 785-1212 (inquiries)
(401) 785-1213 (complaints)

South Carolina

1830 Bull St.
Columbia, SC 29201
(803) 254-2525

311 Pettigru St.
Greenville, SC 29601
(803) 242-5052

P.O. Box 8603
Myrtle Beach, SC 29578-8603
(803) 448-6100

Tennessee

P.O. Box 1176 TCAS
Blountville, TN 37617
(615) 323-6311

1010 Market St., Suite 200
Chattanooga, TN 37402
(615) 266-6144
(615) 479-6096 (Bradley
   County)
(615) 266-6144 (Whitfield and
   Murray counties)

P.O. 10327
Knoxville, TN 37939-0327
(615) 522-2552/2130/2139

P.O. Box 41406
Memphis, TN 38174-1406
(901) 272-9641

One Commerce Pl., Suite 1830
Nashville, TN 37239
(615) 254-5872

Texas

3300 S. 14th St., Suite 307
Abilene, TX 79605
(915) 691-1533

P.O. Box 1905
Amarillo, TX 79106
(806) 358-6222

1005 American Plaza
Austin, TX 78701
(512) 476-1616

P.O. Box 2988
Beaumont, TX 77704
(409) 835-5348

202 Varisco Bldg.
Bryan, TX 77801
(409) 823-8148/8149

4535 S. Padre Island Dr.
Corpus Christi, TX 78411
(512) 854-2892

2001 Bryan St., Suite 850
Dallas, TX 75201
(214) 220-2000

1910 East Yandell
El Paso, TX 79903
(915) 545-1212/1264

106 West Fifth St.
Fort Worth, TX 76102
(817) 332-7585

2707 N. Loop West, Suite 900
Houston, TX 77008
(713) 868-9500

P.O. Box 1178
Lubbock, TX 79401
(806) 763-0459

P.O. Box 60206
Midland, TX 79711
(915) 563-1880
(800) 592-4433 (toll free in TX)

P.O. Box 3366
San Ángelo, TX 76902-3366
(915) 653-2318

1800 Northeast Loop 410, #400
San Antonio, TX 78217
(512) 828-9441

P.O. Box 6652
Tyler, TX 75711-6652
(214) 581-5704

P.O. Box 7203
Waco, TX 76714-7203
(817) 772-7530

P.O. Box 69
Weslaco, TX 78596
(512) 968-3678

1106 Brook Ave.
Wichita Falls, TX 76301
(817) 723-5526

Utah

385 24th St., Suite 717
Ogden, UT 84401
(801) 399-4701

1588 S. Main
Salt Lake City, UT 84115
(801) 487-4656
(801) 377-2611 (Provo)

Virginia

3608 Tidewater Dr.
Norfolk, VA 23509
(804) 627-5651

701 E. Franklin, Suite 712
Richmond, VA 23219
(804) 648-0016

121 W. Campbell Ave. SW
Roanoke, VA 24011
(703) 342-3455

Washington

127 W. Canal Dr.
Kennewick, WA 99336
(509) 582-0222

2200 Sixth Ave., Suite 828
Seattle, WA 98121-1857
(206) 448-8888

S. 176 Stevens St.
Spokane, WA 99204
(509) 747-1155

P.O. Box 1274
Tacoma, WA 98401
(206) 383-5561

P.O. Box 1584
Yakima, WA 98907
(509) 248-1326

Wisconsin

740 N. Plankinton Ave.
Milwaukee, WI 53202
(414) 273-1600 (inquiries)
(414) 273-0123 (complaints)

Wyoming

BBB/Idaho Falls (Lincoln Park
and Teton counties)
(208) 523-9754

BBB/Fort Collins (all other Wyoming counties)
(800) 873-3222 (toll free)

STATE CONSUMER ACTION AGENCIES

This appendix lists state consumer action agencies. If you do not live in or close to the city listed for your state, call the state office or the toll-free number to get a local office referral. Most offices distribute consumer information pamphlets and resolve complaints through mediation or arbitration.

Alabama

Consumer Protection Division
Office of Attorney General
11 S. Union St.
Montgomery, AL 36130
(205) 261-7334
(800) 392-5658 (toll free in AL)

Alaska

Consumer Protection Section
Office of Attorney General
1031 W. 4th Ave., Suite 110-B
Anchorage, AK 99501
(907) 279-0428

Arizona

Financial Fraud Division
Office of Attorney General
1275 W. Washington St.
Phoenix, AZ 85007
(602) 542-3702
(800) 352-8431 (toll free in AZ)

Arkansas

Consumer Protection Division
Office of Attorney General
200 Tower Bldg., 4th & Center
  Sts.
Little Rock, AR 72201
(501) 682-2007
(800) 482-8982 (toll free in AR)

California

Public Inquiry Unit
Office of Attorney General
1515 K St., Suite 511
Sacramento, CA 94244-2550
(916) 322-3360
(800) 952-5225 (toll free in CA)

Consumer Protection Division
Los Angeles City Attorney's Office
200 N. Main St.
1600 City Hall East
Los Angeles, CA 90012
(213) 485-4515

Colorado

Consumer Protection Unit
Office of Attorney General
1525 Sherman St., 3rd Floor
Denver, CO 80203
(303) 866-5167

Connecticut

Department of Consumer Protection
165 Capitol Ave.
Hartford, CT 06106
(203) 566-4999
(800) 842-2649 (toll free in CT)

Delaware

Division of Consumer Affairs
Department of Community Affairs
820 N. French St., 4th Floor
Wilmington, DE 19801
(302) 571-3250

District of Columbia

Department of Consumer & Regulatory Affairs
614 H St. NW
Washington, DC 20001
(202) 727-7000

Florida

Division of Consumer Services
218 Mayo Bldg.
Tallahassee, FL 32399

(904) 488-2226
(800) 342-2176 (toll free in FL)

Georgia

Governor's Office of Consumer Affairs
2 Martin Luther King, Jr. Dr. SE
Plaza Level, E. Tower
Atlanta, GA 30334
(404) 656-7000
(800) 282-5808 (toll free in GA)

Hawaii

Office of Consumer Protection
828 Fort St. Mall
Honolulu, HI 96812-3767
(808) 548-2560/2540

Idaho

None

Illinois

Consumer Protection Division
Office of Attorney General
100 W. Randolph St., 12th Floor
Chicago, IL 60601
(312) 917-3580

Indiana

Consumer Protection Division
Office of Attorney General
219 State House
Indianapolis, IN 46204
(317) 232-6330
(800) 382-5516 (toll free in IN)

Iowa

Consumer Protection Division
Office of Attorney General
1300 E. Walnut St., 2nd Floor
Des Moines, IA 50319
(515) 281-5926

Kansas

Consumer Protection Division
Office of Attorney General
Kansas Judicial Ctr., 2nd Floor
Topeka, KS 66612
(913) 296-3751
(800) 432-2310 (toll free in KS)

Kentucky

Consumer Protection Division
Office of Attorney General
209 St. Clair St.
Frankfort, KY 40601
(502) 564-2200
(800) 432-9257 (toll free in KY)

Louisiana

Consumer Protection Section
Office of Attorney General
State Capitol Bldg., P.O. Box 94005
Baton Rouge, LA 70804
(504) 342-7013

Maine

Consumer and Antitrust Division
Office of Attorney General
State House Station #6
Augusta, ME 04333
(207) 289-3716 (9 A.M.–1 P.M.)

Maryland

Consumer Protection Division
Office of Attorney General
7 N. Calvert St., 3rd Floor
Baltimore, MD 21202
(301) 528-8662 (9 A.M.–2 P.M.)

Massachusetts

Consumer Protection Division
Office of Attorney General
One Ashburton Place, Room 1411
Boston, MA 02108
(617) 727-7780

Michigan

Consumer Protection Division
Office of Attorney General
670 Law Bldg.
Lansing, MI 48913
(517) 373-1140

Minnesota

Office of Consumer Services
Office of Attorney General
117 University Ave.
St. Paul, MN 55155
(612) 296-2331

Mississippi

Consumer Protection Division
Office of Attorney General
P.O. Box 220
Jackson, MS 39205
(601) 359-3680

Missouri

Trade Offense Division
Office of Attorney General
P.O. Box 899
Jefferson City, MO 65102
(314) 751-2616
(800) 392-8222 (toll free in MO)

Montana

Consumer Affairs Unit
Department of Commerce
1424 9th Ave.
Helena, MT 59620
(406) 444-4312

Nebraska

Consumer Protection Division
Department of Justice
2115 State Capitol, P.O. Box
   98920
Lincoln, NE 68509
(402) 471-4723

Nevada

Department of Commerce
State Mail Room Complex
Las Vegas, NV 89158
(702) 486-4150

New Hampshire

Consumer Protection and Anti-
   trust Division
Office of Attorney General
State House Annex
Concord, NH 03301
(603) 271-3641

New Jersey

Division of Consumer Affairs
1100 Raymond Blvd., Room 504
Newark, NJ 07102
(201) 648-4010

New Mexico

Consumer and Economic Crime
   Division
Office of Attorney General
P.O. Box Drawer 1508
Santa Fe, NM 87504
(505) 872-6910
(800) 432-2070 (toll free in NM)

New York

Consumer Protection Board
99 Washington Ave.
Albany, NY 12210
(518) 474-8583

Consumer Protection Board
250 Broadway, 17th Floor
New York, NY 10007-2593
(212) 587-4908

North Carolina

Consumer Protection Section
Office of Attorney General
P.O. Box 629
Raleigh, NC 27602
(919) 733-7741

North Dakota

Consumer Fraud Division
Office of Attorney General
State Capitol Bldg.
Bismarck, ND 58505
(701) 224-2210
(800) 472-2600 (toll free in ND)

Ohio

Consumer Frauds and Crimes
   Section
Office of Attorney General
30 E. Broad St., 25th Floor
Columbus, OH 43266-0410
(614) 466-4986
(800) 282-0515 (toll free in OH)

Oklahoma

Consumer Affairs
Office of Attorney General
112 State Capitol Bldg.
Oklahoma City, OK 73105
(405) 521-3921

Oregon

Financial Fraud Section
Office of Attorney General
Justice Bldg.
Salem, OR 97310
(503) 378-4320

Pennsylvania

Bureau of Consumer Protection
Office of Attorney General
Strawberry Sq., 14th Floor
Harrisburg, PA 17120
(717) 787-9707
(800) 441-2555 (toll free in PA)

Puerto Rico

Department of Consumer Affairs
Minillas Station
P.O. Box 41059
Santurce, PR 00940
(809) 722-7555

Rhode Island

Consumer Protection Division
Department of Attorney General
72 Pine St.
Providence, RI 02903
(401) 277-2104
(800) 852-7776 (toll free in RI)

South Carolina

Department of Consumer Affairs
P.O. Box 5757
Columbia, SC 29250
(803) 734-9452
(800) 922-1594 (toll free in SC)

South Dakota

Division of Consumer Affairs
Office of Attorney General
State Capitol Bldg.
Pierre, SD 57501
(605) 773-4400

Tennessee

Division of Consumer Affairs
Department of Commerce & Insurance
500 James Robertson Pkwy., 5th Floor
Nashville, TN 37219
(615) 741-4737
(800) 342-8385 (toll free in TN)

Texas

Consumer Protection Division
Office of Attorney General
Box 12548, Capitol Station
Austin, TX 78711
(512) 463-2070

Utah

Division of Consumer Protection
Department of Business Regulation
160 E. Third South
P.O. Box 45802
Salt Lake City, UT 84145
(801) 530-6601

Vermont

Public Protection Division
Office of Attorney General
109 State St.
Montpelier, VT 05602
(802) 828-3171

Virgin Islands

Department of Licensing and Consumer Affairs
Property and Procurement Bldg.
Subbase #1, Room 205
St. Thomas, VI 0801
(809) 774-3130

Virginia

Division of Consumer Counsel
Office of Attorney General
Supreme Court Bldg.
101 N. 8th St.
Richmond, VA 23219
(804) 786-2116

Washington

Consumer and Business Fair
  Practices Division
710 2nd Ave., Suite 1300
Seattle, WA 98104
(206) 464-7744
(800) 551-4636 (toll free in WA)

West Virginia

Consumer Protection Division
Office of Attorney General
812 Quarrier St., 6th Floor
Charleston, WV 25301
(304) 348-8986
(800) 368-8808 (toll free in WV)

Wisconsin

Office of Consumer Protection
Department of Justice
P.O. Box 7856
Madison, WI 53707
(608) 266-1852
(800) 362-8189 (toll free in WI)

Wyoming

Office of Attorney General
123 State Capitol Bldg.
Cheyenne, WY 82002
(307) 777-6286

GLOSSARY OF TERMS

The following terms are used in this book. Italicized terms in definitions are themselves defined in other entries.

Answer   *Defendant*'s formal written statement of defense against the *plaintiff*'s complaint in a lawsuit. The answer addresses the truth or falsity of the plaintiff's claims and can include a *counterclaim*.

Appeal   Request that a higher court review the decision of a lower court to correct errors in the application of law or procedure.

Arbitration   Method of settling disputes in which the two sides submit arguments to a neutral third party or panel, which makes a decision after listening to both sides and considering the evidence.

Assignee   Person to whom a right or interest is given or transferred. In small claims court, a party to a lawsuit may decide to transfer his or her right or interest in that lawsuit to another person (the assignee).

Attachment   Method by which real or personal property is legally taken by a creditor and held pending the outcome of a lawsuit over a debt.

Class action   Lawsuit brought by one or more individuals on behalf of a larger group of individuals in the same legal situation.

Compulsory counterclaim   *Counterclaim* in which the *defendant*'s claim against the *plaintiff* arises out of the same transaction or occurrence as in the original complaint. The defendant must file a counterclaim in that lawsuit or forever be barred from raising that claim in a separate lawsuit.

Continuance   Postponement of a legal proceeding or deadline.

Counterclaim Claim made by a *defendant* in a civil lawsuit that, in effect, sues the *plaintiff* (see *Permissive counterclaim* and *Compulsory counterclaim*).

Crossclaim Claim litigated by codefendants or coplaintiffs against each other and not against persons on the opposite side of the lawsuit.

Default judgment Decision in favor of the *plaintiff* because the *defendant* failed to respond to the plaintiff's complaint within the time required by law, or failed to appear in court on the scheduled date of the hearing or trial.

Defendant Person against whom a legal action is filed.

Deposition Out-of-court process of taking the sworn testimony of a witness. This is usually done by a lawyer with a lawyer from the other side being permitted to attend or participate. The purpose is to disclose relevant information so that each side can evaluate its case before going to trial and decide whether to pursue the claim or settle out of court.

Detainer Holding a person against his or her will, or keeping a person from goods or land he or she legally owns.

Discovery Before-trial formal and informal exchange of information between the sides in a lawsuit. Two types of discovery are *interrogatories* and *depositions.*

Eminent domain Government's right to take private property for public use simply by paying for it.

Equity Principles of fairness and justice. In small claims courts that allow "equitable relief," judges are allowed to order a party to do something other than payment of money damages (see *Rescission, Restitution, Reformation* and *Specific performance*).

Forcible entry and detainer Court proceeding that restores land or property to one who is wrongfully kept out or deprived of legal possession.

Garnishment Legal proceeding in which a debtor's wages, property, money or credits are taken to satisfy payment of a debt or *judgment.*

Injunction Judge's order to do or to refrain from doing a specified thing. For example, a court might issue an injunction ordering a landlord to restore heat to a tenant's apartment even though the tenant's rent is overdue.

Interrogatory Form of *discovery* in which written questions posed by one side in a lawsuit require written responses under oath by the other.

Judgment   Final decision announced or written by a judge about the rights and claims of each side in a lawsuit.

Judgment creditor   Person to whom money is owed after a court's *judgment.*

Judgment debtor   Person who owes money after a court's *judgment.*

Libel   False or malicious written statements that injure a person's reputation, business or property rights.

Lien   Legal claim to hold or sell property as security for a debt.

Mediation   Informal alternative to suing in which both sides to a dispute meet with a neutral third party (mediator) to negotiate a resolution. The resolution is usually put into a written agreement that is signed by both sides.

Negotiable instrument   Signed document containing an unconditional promise to pay an exact sum of money on demand or at a specified time. It must be marked, payable "to the order of" or "to the bearer." Examples are checks, notes and certificates of deposit.

Order   Written command by a judge or court clerk describing a decision of the court, directing or forbidding an action, or issuing the final ruling of the court in a case.

Permissive counterclaim   *Counterclaim* in which the *defendant*'s claim against the *plaintiff* is unrelated to the claims stated in the original complaint. It is "permissive" in that if the defendant doesn't counterclaim, he or she may still bring an individual lawsuit.

Plaintiff   Person who files a lawsuit against another.

Pleading   Making a formal written statement of the claims or defenses of each side in a lawsuit.

Prejudgment detainer   Court *order* to hold property or personal goods until a final court decision is made.

Reformation   Equitable remedy in which a court rewrites, corrects or amends a written agreement to conform with the original intent of the parties to that agreement.

Rescission   Equitable remedy in which a court cancels a contract. For instance, if a judge finds that a contract is unfair or fraudulent, he or she may decide to cancel (rescind) the contract and act as if it had never existed.

Restitution   Equitable remedy in which something is ordered given back or made good on. For instance, a judge may order that a *plaintiff* be put back in the financial position he or she was in before entering a contract.

Service   Delivery of a legal document by an officially authorized person to meet formal requirements of the applicable laws and assure that the person being sued is formally notified about the lawsuit or other legal action.

Slander   False or malicious oral statements that injure a person's reputation, business or property rights.

Specific performance   Equitable remedy in which a court requires a party to do something. For example, a judge may order that a one-of-a-kind object be returned to its original owner.

Statute of limitations   Law that sets a deadline for filing a lawsuit. This varies from state to state and with the basis of the lawsuit.

Transfer   Procedure by which a *defendant* can have a case moved to a higher court.

Venue   Place where a case may be tried. A court may have the power to take a case within a wide geographic area, but the proper venue for the case may be one place within that area.

Writ of execution   Court *order* allowing a sheriff, marshal or other official to collect money or property owed by the *judgment debtor.*

BIBLIOGRAPHY

Collect Your Court Judgment, by Gini Graham Scott, Stephen Elias and Lisa Goldoftas. Nolo Press, 950 Parker St., Berkeley, CA 94710. 1988 (1st Ed.). $24.95.

Guide to collecting court judgments in California—whether from small claims, municipal or superior court. Step-by-step instructions and forms used to collect judgments from a debtor's bank accounts, wages, business receipts, real estate and other assets.

Everybody's Guide to Small Claims Court, by Ralph Warner. Nolo Press, 950 Parker St., Berkeley, CA 94710. 1987 (national 3rd Ed.). $14.95.

Step-by-step "how-to" book illustrated with true-to-life examples. Sample forms for New York and California's small claims courts included along with information compiled in 1987 for all fifty states is also included.

Everybody's Guide to Small Claims Court, by Ralph Warner. Nolo Press, 950 Parker St., Berkeley, CA 94710. 1987 (California 7th Ed.). $14.95.

Specifically for California residents, with much of the same information, examples and California forms in national edition.

How You Can Sue Without Hiring a Lawyer, by John Striker and Andrew Shapiro. Simon and Schuster, 1230 6th Ave., New York, NY. 10020. 1981. (Out of print.)

Attorneys John Striker and Andrew Shapiro advise you to defer to or consult with lawyers often. Nevertheless, this helpful book devotes equal space to describing process and applying it to wide variety of legal problems.

Inexpensive Justice: Self Representation in the Small Claims Court, by Robert L. Spurrier, Jr. Associated Faculty Press, Inc., Route 100, Millwood, NY. 10546. 1983. $12.95.

Excellent but expensive resource book. Its fewer than 100 pages can be read in one sitting. Does not include information on mediation or arbitration.

Small Claims Court Guide for Washington, by Donald D. Stuart. Self-Counsel Press Inc., 1303 N. Northgate Way, Seattle, WA, 98133. 1989 (2d Ed.). $8.95.

Useful guide for residents of Washington with instructions on successfully filing or defending a case in small claims court, appealing a decision and collecting your judgment. Twenty-one sample forms used in Washington's small claims court.

Sue the B*st*rds: The Victim's Handbook Newly Revised and Updated, by Douglas Matthews. Arbor House Publishing Co., 235 E. 45th St. New York, NY. 10017. 1981. (Out of print.)

Although text written in 1973, book still offers useful tips but because laws governing small claims courts change frequently, the state rules appendices, most recently revised in 1981, are no longer up to date. Available only through local libraries and law libraries.

The People's Court: How to Tell It to the Judge, by Harvey Levin, William Morrow & Co., 105 Madison Ave., New York, NY 18016. $4.95. 1985.

Impressive array of cases from television courtroom of Judge Joseph Wapner's *People's Court.* Cases bear catchy names like "The Munched-on Mailman" and "Looking for Love in All the Wrong Places." Particularly helpful is Levin's explanation of how Judge Wapner arrives at his decisions.

About the Author

Theresa Meehan Rudy is a program specialist with HALT—An Organization of Americans For Legal Reform. She has contributed to HALT's library of educational materials as author of *Fee Arbitration: Model Rules and Commentary* and as a coauthor of *Everyday Contracts: Protecting Your Rights.* Ms. Rudy also serves as a lay arbitrator for the District of Columbia Bar's fee arbitration program. She holds a B.A., cum laude, from the University of Massachusetts, Amherst.